*Earl of Devonshire, Marquis of Hartington, Baron of Hardwick, L.d Stewa*r*d*
&c Trent North and K.t of the Most Noble Order of the Garter —

17

THE HOUSE
A PORTRAIT OF CHATSWORTH

Colossal foot, *c.* first century B.C., long thought to be spurious,
now known to be one of a pair from a giant female figure

THE HOUSE

A PORTRAIT OF

CHATSWORTH

BY

The Duchess of Devonshire

'Reading is a pernicious habit. It
destroys all originality of sentiment.'
Thomas Hobbes
(1588–1679)
Tutor of The Second and Third Earls of Devonshire

M

MACMILLAN   LONDON

ISBN 0 333 28455 0

First published 1982 by
Macmillan London Limited
London and Basingstoke
Reprinted 1982, 1983

Associated companies in Auckland, Dallas,
Delhi, Dublin, Hong Kong, Johannesburg,
Lagos, Manzini, Melbourne, Nairobi,
New York, Singapore, Tokyo, Washington
and Zaria

Printed in Great Britain by
BAS Printers Limited, Over Wallop, Hampshire

To Andrew

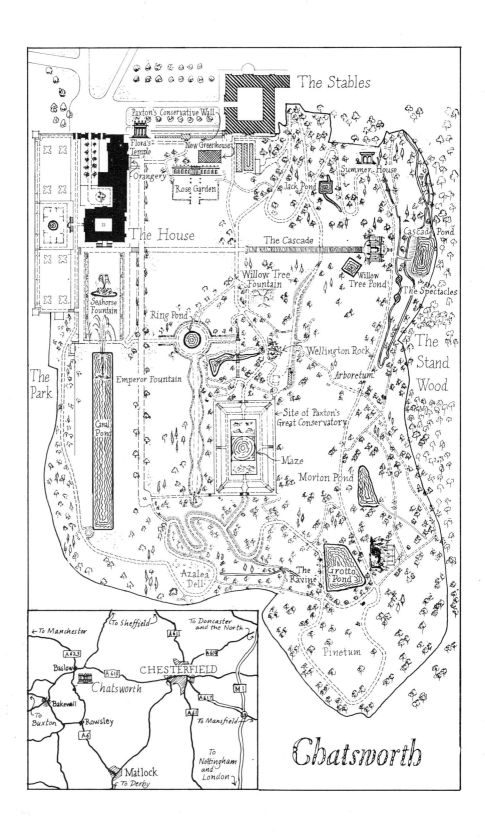

Contents

List of Illustrations

Sixteen of the colour illustrations and eighteen of those in black and white are reproduced from photographs specially taken for this book by Christopher Barker. The rest are from the Chatsworth collection or lent by former staff.

The Cavendish Family

1505–1557 Sir William Cavendish ⊤ Bess of Hardwick c1527–1608
son of Thomas Cavendish of Suffolk | later Countess of Shrewsbury

1552–1625 William Cavendish ⊤ Anne Keighley –1625
1st Earl of Devonshire (1618) | dau of Henry Keighley

1590–1628 William Cavendish ⊤ Hon. Christian Bruce 1595–1675
2nd Earl of Devonshire | dau of 1st Lord Kinloss

1617–1684 William Cavendish ⊤ Lady Elizabeth Cecil 1619–1689
3rd Earl of Devonshire | dau of the Earl of Salisbury

1640–1707 William Cavendish ⊤ Lady Mary Butler 1646–1710
4th Earl of Devonshire | dau of the Duke of Ormonde
1st Duke of Devonshire (1694)

1673–1729 William Cavendish ⊤ Hon. Rachel Russell 1674–1725
2nd Duke of Devonshire | dau of William Lord Russell

1698–1755 William Cavendish ⊤ Catherine Hoskins –1777   Lord Charles Cavendish ⊤ Anne Grey –1733
3rd Duke of Devonshire | dau of John Hoskins | dau of the Duke of Kent
                                                              1731–1810 Henry Cavendish the scientist

1720–1764 William Cavendish ⊤ Lady Charlotte Boyle 1731–1754
4th Duke of Devonshire | dau of 4th Earl of Cork and 3rd Earl of Burlington, estates in Yorkshire and Ireland, Chiswick House, Burlington House

1757–1806 (1) Lady Georgiana Spencer ⊤ William Cavendish 1748–1811 ⊤ (2) Lady Elizabeth Hervey afterwards Foster 1759–1824   1754–1834 George Cavendish ⊤ Lady Elizabeth Compton 1760–1835
dau of the Earl Spencer | 5th Duke of Devonshire | dau of the Earl of Bristol   1st Earl of Burlington (2nd creation) | heiress to the Earls of Northampton
                                                                                                                                                                  estates in Sussex

1790–1858 William Spencer Cavendish ⊤ Lady Georgiana Cavendish   George Howard 1773–1848 ⊤   1783–1812 William Cavendish ⊤ Hon. Louisa O'Callaghan –1863
6th Duke of Devonshire   1783–1858   6th Earl of Carlisle   killed in carriage accident | dau of Lord Lismore

1803–1881 Lady Caroline Howard ⊤ Hon. William Lascelles 1798–1851   1812–1840 Lady Blanche Howard ⊤ William Cavendish 1808–1891
                                 son of the Earl of Harewood   2nd Earl of Burlington (2nd creation)
                                                                                                               7th Duke of Devonshire

1838–1920 Emma Lascelles ⊤ Lord Edward Cavendish 1838–1891   1833–1908 Spencer Compton Cavendish ⊤ Louise von Alten 1832–1911
                                                              8th Duke of Devonshire | Duchess of Manchester

1868–1938 Victor Cavendish ⊤ Lady Evelyn Fitzmaurice 1870–1960
9th Duke of Devonshire | dau of the Marquess of Lansdowne 'Granny Evie'

1895–1950 Edward Cavendish ⊤ Lady Mary Cecil 1895–
10th Duke of Devonshire | dau of the Marquess of Salisbury 'Moucher'

1920– Andrew Cavendish ⊤ Hon. Deborah Mitford 1920–   1917–1944 William Cavendish ⊤ Kathleen Kennedy 1920–1948
11th Duke of Devonshire | dau of Lord Redesdale   Marquess of Hartington | sister of President Kennedy
                                                           killed in action

1944– Peregrine Cavendish ⊤ Amanda Heywood-Lonsdale 1944–   1943– Lady Emma Cavendish ⊤ Hon. Tobias Tennant   1957– Lady Sophia Cavendish ⊤ Anthony Murphy
Marquess of Hartington | son of Lord Glenconner

1969– William Cavendish   1971– Lady Celina Cavendish   1973– Lady Jasmine Cavendish   1964– Isabel Tennant   1967– Edward Tennant   1970– Stella Tennant
Earl of Burlington

Acknowledgements

I have many people to thank for their help with this book.

It never would have been written if Uncle Harold Macmillan had not suggested it.

Andrew and the Trustees of the Chatsworth Settlement agreed to the reprinting of some of the Bachelor Duke's *Handbook*.

Andrew allowed me to re-arrange the house in the 1950s, and together we planned the new plantings in the garden.

There would be no house to write about if it were not for the people who look after it.

The late Willie Shimwell devoted his life to it. He answered my questions about Granny Evie's time and a hundred other things with great patience. Dennis Fisher, who succeeded him as comptroller and understands how things work above and below ground, did the same. Ash Withers, engineer and assistant comptroller, counted the rooms and the windows and walked the course to ensure accuracy in space and distance. Bob Getty, clerk of works, measured the air enclosed by the walls. Tony Hubbock, electrician, counted the electric light bulbs.

Mrs Willie Shimwell, Mrs Jesse Grafton, Mrs Billy Bond, Mrs Sidney Child, Mrs Len Barnes and Henry Bennett allowed me to print their recollections of working in the house in the twenties and thirties, and have lent me photographs.

Peter Day, keeper of the collections, and Michael Pearman, librarian, have done research for me and come up with the answers in double-quick time.

Bert Link, head gardener from 1939 to 1974, reminded me of the work we have done in the garden.

Jackie Allen and Rosemary Marchant typed the messy manuscript. I thank them, and people in the Estate Office, for finding facts and figures. I am deeply grateful to Eric Oliver, comptroller, who always says 'yes' to impossible requests, Mrs Dean, housekeeper now retired, and her successor, Christine Tindale, whose standards are the highest, Mrs Carr, head housemaid, and Henry Coleman, butler, who make difficult things seem easy, Jean-Pierre Beraud, chef, whose cooking put me in a good temper for over two years, Maud Barnes, maid, who resisted throwing away unlikely-looking bits of paper which strung the thing together, and all the rest of the staff, both indoors and out, without whom we could not live here.

When Uncle Harold asked me to get on with it he knew Richard Garnett would be a shoulder to lean on. He wrote, 'In all this I feel like the Chairman of the Board of Governors of the B.B.C., Garnett is the producer, and you are the prima donna.' I don't know about being a prima donna, but Richard Garnett is a producer in a million.

View from the south-east, showing the river Derwent and Paine's bridge, the canal pond, serpentine hedge and maze

Introduction

Not a palace, not a castle, not a museum, but a house—always called 'the house'. 'I'll come across to the house', 'See you at the house at 9.30', 'I think he's somewhere in the house', 'They're going round the house', a constant reminder of what the huge building is for: a place for people to live in.

Chatsworth is in a valley in the Peak District of Derbyshire, high up and in the middle of England. It is a very big house in a very big valley, with a steep and wooded hill behind, a river in front, encompassed by a large garden and even larger park: the usual receipt for an English country house.

But there is a quality about the place which makes it out of the ordinary. Perhaps the giant scale has something to do with it, or perhaps it is the scenery; a classic mixture of wild and domestic: moor, rocks and bracken descending through woods to grazing land and quiet riverside.

When you arrive in the park on the public road you take in this rare variety of scene in one glance, and as the road winds through hill and valley the eye is inevitably drawn towards the house; glimpses long enough to give an impression of the country and what it contains, and short enough to make you curious to see more.

The house looks permanent; as permanent as if it had been there, not for a few hundred years, but for ever. It fits its landscape exactly. The river is the right distance away and the right width. The bridge is at a comfortable angle for leaning on and gazing from. The stone from which the house is built comes out of the ground nearby, and so it is the proper colour, on the bird's nest theory of building materials being at hand and of the place, and therefore right for the surroundings.

As you leave the public road at Sandy's Turn the west front of the house appears over the river, and from this point the Sixth Duke's long west garden wall. Above it and parallel to the south front the cascade gives movement and a liveliness that only fast-moving water can. Higher up in the wood are two tall waterfalls—one straight off the aqueduct, the other crooked over rocks, and the Emperor Fountain in the canal rises like a plume of agitated white smoke.

The stables on the hillside are built of enormous rusticated stones and are of perfect proportion with a grandly high coved ceiling over the covered ride through the arch. Higher still, the Elizabethan hunting tower stands guard.

All there is to be seen appears to have arrived by nature as though it fell into place without effort, and the ease and pleasure with which the eye takes it in underlines this feeling of accident rather than design. The highest compliment which can be paid about any new work done in the house, garden or park is to say it looks as if it had always been there. When the long wing was built with the high belvedere tower on the end people cannot have thought that it looked as if it had always been there, but after a hundred and fifty years even this has bedded in and begins to take on the same feeling of permanence as the main square block.

From inside the house the pleasure of looking out is intense. There is not an ugly thing to be seen. No telephone or electric poles have been allowed to obtrude on the landscape to vex the eye.

The rim of the park is planted in wedge-shaped blocks of trees, so that when one block is mature and ready to be cut down there is another growing up to take its place. This distant enclosure gives an impression of a secure place beyond which the unknown world may be ugly and badly arranged, but within the magic boundary all is well.

It has taken more than four hundred years to reach this apparently effortless state of perfection by a combination of luck and good management. The luck is that every generation of Cavendishes has loved and respected the house and its surroundings, and each has added something to it, and the good management is literally so in that no house has been better served by its stewards and housekeepers than has Chatsworth.

To understand how it came about it is necessary to inflict on the reader a few words about the family and its history. It is so intertwined with that of the house and its contents that to write the story of the building and the rooms without a brief mention of the earlier Cavendishes would be to leave out the core of the matter.

Chatsworth from Paine's bridge

The Cascade from under the steps on the south front

PART ONE

The History of the House

Elizabethan Chatsworth by Richard Wilson after Siberechts

Early History

Sir William Cavendish (*b.* 1505) of Cavendish in Suffolk, descendant of the slayer of Wat Tyler, was Treasurer of the Chamber to King Henry VIII and King Edward VI, and benefited greatly by the distribution of abbey lands at the dissolution of the monasteries. He married Elizabeth Hardwick in 1547. He was the second of her four husbands and the only one by whom she had children. 'Bess of Hardwick' was born in Derbyshire about 1527, and by the time she married William Cavendish she was already a considerable landowner in that county, through inheritance from her father and her first husband. This fascinating and forceful woman persuaded Sir William to sell his land in Suffolk, and in 1549 he bought properties in Derbyshire, including the land on which Chatsworth stands.

It was wild country, hard and desolate. The rocky heights behind the site of the new house carried few trees, and the river Derwent was prone to sudden and dangerous flooding. Two hundred years later, Defoe could still describe the moor you had to cross when travelling from Chesterfield or Sheffield as a 'waste and howling wilderness with neither

Bess of Hardwick (*c.* 1527–1608)

Sir William Cavendish (1505–1557)

19

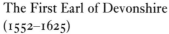

The First Earl of Devonshire
(1552–1625)

The Second Earl of Devonshire
(1590–1628)

hedge, house nor tree over which when strangers travel they are obliged to take guides or it would be next to impossible not to lose the way'.

In 1552, undeterred by the physical difficulties of the site, Sir William and Bess started to build a big house where the square building stands now. There is a painting of their house with its pretty gazebos and entrance lodges, so we know what it looked like outside, but there is nothing to tell us about the inside. Some of the Elizabethan walls survive, embedded in the classicised house you see today. In those days the village of Edensor occupied the valley where the public and private roads join, and straggled on south past the foundations of the old bridge just above the weir on the curve of the river.

In 1557, five years after the building was begun, Sir William died, leaving Bess with six surviving children, of whom their second son, William, became their heir. Bess's fourth and last marriage to the Earl of Shrewsbury took place in 1568. Lord Shrewsbury was chosen by Queen Elizabeth I to be custodian of Mary Queen of Scots, and several times while in his care she was an unwilling guest at Chatsworth. Her lodgings were on the east side of the house, and although they are changed beyond recognition, the rooms there are still known as the Queen of Scots Apartments.

The curious moated building near the bridge is called Queen Mary's Bower, and the legend that the unfortunate Queen was allowed to take the air there is probably true. At that time it was enclosed by the garden walls and was reasonably safe from any attempt at rescue, which was Lord Shrewsbury's constant fear.

The Third Earl of Devonshire (1617–1684)

Thomas Hobbes (1588–1679)

Bess died, aged 81, in 1608, having amassed large estates and built three major houses—Chatsworth, Oldcotes and lastly her extraordinary masterpiece, Hardwick Hall, the only one which survives as she built it.

Her son, Sir William Cavendish (*b.* 1552) succeeded her and was created Baron Cavendish in 1605 and Earl of Devonshire in 1618. He died in 1625. Thomas Hobbes (1588–1679), philosopher, political theorist and author of the *Leviathan*, was appointed tutor to William, the Second Earl, and stayed with the family, off and on, for the rest of his life.

William, Second Earl (1590–1628), married Christian Bruce, daughter of Lord Kinloss, and they had two sons, William, who became Third Earl, and Charles who was killed fighting on the side of the King in the Civil War.

William, Third Earl (1617–1684), although Royalist by inclination, lived up to the family motto of 'Safety with caution' and stayed out of the country while Chatsworth was occupied by both sides in the Civil War. When peace and calm returned with the Restoration, the Third Earl of Devonshire reconstructed the principal rooms in an attempt to make them more comfortable and up-to-date. It was done in a haphazard way, the height of the building was too much for the foundations, cracks appeared, and it became unsafe. The clerk of works pronounced it to be 'decaying and weake', and so in 1686, two years after he succeeded, the Fourth Earl began his great work of rebuilding.

The First Eight Dukes

The Fourth Earl and First Duke, William (1640–1707)

It is Chatsworth's great good fortune that the rebuilding of the old house was done at a time (1686–1707) when it was impossible to invent anything ugly. There is ample evidence of this in all the work done by the First Duke. The design of each side of the square block, the style, proportions and decoration, both inside and out, and the shape of the garden, reflect all that was best in the golden age of architecture and the embellishment of a great building and its immediate surroundings.

The Duke (who was given his title in 1694 for his part in bringing William of Orange to the English throne) got into a scrape in London over a matter of a fine of £30,000 for tweaking the nose of a certain Colonel Culpepper, and so he hurried to Chatsworth till the trouble blew over. There he had the time and the inclination to start work on the old house. He began by altering the south front, which was all he meant to do. But he found building so delightful that he set about the east front in 1691, and then made the west, finishing the north just before he died in 1707. William Talman was his architect for the south and east. Thomas Archer may have been responsible for the west and north, but it is thought that the Duke himself had a large hand in it. Stables and offices were rebuilt on their old site to the north-west of the house.

The transformation of the garden was no less dramatic. It became a horticultural complement to the architecture of the newly classicised house, a sharply defined and ordered plot, formal and exact, an artificial wonder in complete contrast to the wild Peak country which contained it.

The Duke, advised by London and Wise, planted avenues and parterres, levelled a bowling green and gave it a house like a Greek temple, created fountains and a greenhouse. A Frenchman, Grillet, was commissioned to build the cascade and Thomas Archer to design the 'house' from which it springs. Most ambitious of all, the Duke caused a

The Fourth Earl and First Duke of
Devonshire (1640–1707)

The Second Duke of Devonshire
(1673–1729)

hill which was in the way of the view to the south, to be removed, and a
canal, 314 yards long, to be dug in its place (1702). By this time the
tamed and sophisticated beauty of Chatsworth house and gardens must
have presented an astonishing surprise to the traveller passing through
the rugged northern country, and was aptly described by Defoe as being
like a 'fine picture in a dirty grotto'.

The Second Duke, William (1673–1729)

Not surprisingly, the Second Duke made no changes to the wonderful
house and garden he inherited from his father, but he made an
immensely important contribution to Chatsworth in another way.

Passionately fond of drawings and paintings it was he who bought
the group of Dutch and Italian drawings from N. A. Flinck, and Claude's
Liber Veritatis (the artist's record in drawings of his paintings). It is
thought he also added the prints and engravings, and probably (though
it is not certain whether it was he or his father) the Old Master drawings
from the Lankrink and Lely collections. He bought the carved Greek

and Roman antique gems and a collection of coins, as well as many paintings.

The Second Duke was the grandfather of Henry Cavendish (1731–1810) the eminent scientist and great eccentric, whose manuscripts and library of scientific and other books are at Chatsworth, each one stamped with 'H. Cavendish' on the back of the title-page.

Some of the instruments he used for experiments are in the house. Henry was intensely shy and hardly ever spoke. Lord Brougham wrote of meetings of the Royal Society and 'the shrill cry he uttered as he shuffled quickly from room to room. He probably spoke fewer words in the course of his life than any man who ever lived to fourscore years, not excepting the monks of la Trappe.'

The Third Duke, William (1698–1755)

The Third Duke, 'plain in his manners, negligent in his dress', was a Member of Parliament from 1721 till his father's death in 1729, and served for seven years as Lord Lieutenant of Ireland. When Devonshire House in Piccadilly was burnt down in 1733 he commissioned William Kent to rebuild it. Kent also designed furniture for the house, much of which is now at Chatsworth.

The Duke was the lucky recipient of a splendid present given to him by the son of Sir Robert Walpole, the Prime Minister: Van Dyck's portraits of Arthur Goodwin and Jeanne de Blois which hang in the Great Dining-Room.

The Duke was married to one Catherine Hoskins, who, unlike most of the wives of former Cavendishes, had no aristocratic pretensions. Horace Walpole wrote of her, 'The Duchess of Devonshire was more delightfully vulgar than you can imagine: complained of the wet night and how the men would dirty the rooms with their shoes, called out at supper to the Duke, "Good God, my Lord, don't cut the ham—nobody will eat any!" '

They had four sons and three daughters, whose nicknames were Mrs Hopeful, Mrs Tiddle, Guts and Gundy; Puss, Cat and Toe.

The Third Duke of Devonshire
(1698–1755)

The Fourth Duke of Devonshire
(1720–1764)

The Fourth Duke, William (1720–1764)

The Fourth Duke succeeded in 1755. Fashion had changed in the half-century which had passed since the inspired work done at Chatsworth by his great-grandfather, and the Fourth Duke proceeded to make sweeping changes, all except one of which were wonderfully successful. He determined, rightly, that the west should be the front of the house and so he pulled down the old stables and offices which interfered with the approach and employed James Paine to be his architect for new stables (c. 1760) up the slope to the north-east. The course of the river was altered and Paine designed a new bridge (1762). Many of the houses of Edensor which could be seen from Chatsworth were pulled down and the land to the west of the bridge, and what remained of the village, was enclosed to become the park as it is today. (After further changes, the Sixth Duke rebuilt the village in 1834.)

All these changes were for the better: the stables and the bridge are perfect in position, scale, shape and decoration. Had the Duke stopped there one could only have had praise for his alterations and new building, but, alas, the influence of fashion is very strong, and the new idea of 'natural' landscape persuaded him to engage Lancelot 'Capability' Brown to wreck the First Duke's garden.

25

The Stables, *c.* 1760, architect, James Paine

Under Brown's direction terraces turned into slopes, parterres regressed into lawns, many of the ponds and fountains were destroyed, and the west garden became plain grass down to the river, leaving Cibber's sphinxes in stark isolation. The First Duke's bowling house and greenhouse were pulled down and rebuilt on new sites, and the garden took on the shape it is today.

Destructive as he was when let loose in a formal garden surrounding a house, Brown was peerless as a designer of English parks, and this part of his contract was carried out in great style with the supreme confidence of the master of his art. He emphasised the natural lie of the land by plantings of hardwoods and made 'The Duke of Devonshire's Elysian fields' into a place of glorious beauty.

I never cease to marvel at the imagination of his grand designs for large spaces, for the trees took a hundred and fifty to two hundred years to realise the effect he wished to make. Our parents' generation and our own have had the luck to live at the right time to see them at their best.

The Fourth Duke's marriage to Lady Charlotte Boyle, daughter and heiress of the architect Third Earl of Burlington, brought huge new possessions to the Cavendishes, including Bolton Abbey and Londesborough in Yorkshire, Lismore Castle in County Waterford, Chiswick House and Burlington House in London, together with their contents and Lord Burlington's incomparable collection of architectural books and drawings.

26

The Fifth Duke of
Devonshire (1748–1811)

Charlotte died when she was only twenty-three, before her husband
succeeded, but she left four children of whom the eldest, William, was the
Fifth Duke.

The Fifth Duke, William (1748–1811)

The Fifth Duke's chief contribution to Chatsworth was to marry Lady
Georgiana Spencer (famous for her charm, gambling debts, enormous
hats and electioneering prowess) and to father the Sixth Duke—the
'Bachelor Duke'.

The Devonshires lived mostly in London, but when they came to
Chatsworth they filled the house with friends and relations, politicians
and writers. Curiously enough they used the least attractive rooms in
the house, facing north and west.

In spite of his extraordinary indolence he made some alterations to the
house as well as building the beautiful crescent in Buxton. For these
commissions he engaged Carr of York. The small room on the first floor

Lady Georgiana Spencer (1757–1806) wife of the Fifth Duke, and their daughter Georgiana

Lady Elizabeth Foster (1759–1824)

next to the Chapel and its larger neighbour were knocked into one and a new chimney constructed to make what is now the Blue Drawing-Room. Carr was responsible for some of the decoration and furniture. He used the unmistakable small, finicky and ladylike scale of pattern fashionable at that date, usually loosely associated with Robert Adam.

Georgiana commissioned the Frenchmen, François Hervé and Guillaume Gaubert, to make sets of chairs, footstools, sofas and tables, some of which are in the Yellow Drawing-Room, and the rest scattered round the house.

The Duke and his brother, Lord Richard Cavendish, were painted by Pompeo Batoni, the most fashionable portrait-painter of the day. Georgiana was painted several times by Sir Joshua Reynolds, and there is a portrait by the same artist of Lady Elizabeth Foster, Georgiana's great friend who was her husband's mistress and the third member of the curiously contented *ménage à trois* about which so much has been written.

Georgiana died in 1806. After an interval of three and a half years, the Duke married Elizabeth Foster, who was already the mother of two of his children. He died in 1811, and his widow went to live in Rome.

The Sixth Duke of Devonshire
(1790–1858)

The Sixth Duke, William Spencer (1790–1858)

William Spencer Compton, the only son of the Fifth Duke and
Georgiana, called Hart by his family and always known by his successors
as the Bachelor Duke, inherited Chatsworth and all the aforementioned
houses, together with nearly 200,000 acres of land in England and
Ireland, at the age of twenty-one.

His *Handbook to Chatsworth and Hardwick*, written in 1844, reveals
much of himself. His writing shows his love of Chatsworth and his
enthusiasm for all he did there. It describes what he admired; what he
changed and why he changed it, the things he bought and the things he
gave away. It reveals the mixture of grandeur and humility in his
character, of pride of ownership and extreme liberalism in his wish to
share the enjoyment of his possessions with anyone who might be passing.
His generosity and keen appreciation of work done for him by his

29

employees, his delight when a new wonder was added to the many already at Chatsworth, his passionate interest in building and gardening, the intense satisfaction of the great years of creation with Joseph Paxton, and the descriptions of family, guests, servants and neighbours bring the first half of the nineteenth century at Chatsworth vividly to life. But it is his sense of humour which makes one love him more than all the rest put together. He was funny and sad, the irresistible combination which is one of the secrets of charm.

He was the great panjandrum of hosts. His embassy to the coronation of Tsar Nicholas in Moscow in 1825 (which cost him £50,000 more than the sum allowed by the government) was famous for its splendour, and his entertainments in Derbyshire, London and Ireland were no less magnificent.

Princess Victoria came to stay at Chatsworth in 1832, and later when she was Queen in 1843. He gave many a ball and rout at Devonshire House and Chiswick, taking immense trouble to make his guests enjoy themselves. The pleasure he gave at Lismore when the tradespeople of the town and the local gentry of County Waterford dined and danced in the newly-restored Castle, furnished and decorated by Pugin, and illuminated by flares, in 1849, 1850 and 1851, is recorded by their letters of thanks and newspaper cuttings still on the table in the drawing-room there.

The Duke was unusual for a Cavendish in that he was not a politician, although he interested himself in Irish questions, keenly supported the Reform Bill of 1832 and was a willing champion of anyone he thought unjustly treated. Neither, after a short spell as Lord Chamberlain, did he wish to be a courtier.

His life, his work and his pleasure were taken up with Chatsworth and the other houses, and with his friends. Why he never married is a great mystery. Enormously rich and equally charming, he must have been the despair of many an ambitious mother of hopeful daughters. Some say the reason is that he was deaf. Surely that cannot be so, for many deaf men are married. And if he was so deaf, why did he keep a private orchestra? Why was he painted by Landseer in his box at the opera? And how was it that the night before he died 'he sat listening to the playing of Mr Coote, his pianist, beating time with his foot'? Some say he was so much in love with Princess Charlotte that he never wished to marry anyone else. To be faithful to the grave is the ultimate height of romantic love, but so rare as to be very unlikely indeed. The mystery of his bachelorhood remains unsolved.

He was a lonely man and specially so after the death of his niece, Blanche Howard, Countess of Burlington, to whom he was devoted and for whom he planned so much. She married his heir in 1829 and died, aged twenty-nine, in 1840, 'the year of my sorrow', he wrote.

The Bachelor's influence on Chatsworth was immense, and his benign and generous nature pervades the place to this day. You cannot go far, inside or out of doors, without being aware of him.

I shall say no more about him here, for in due course we will follow him round the house with his book as our guide.

The Seventh Duke, William (1808–1891)

In 1858 the Bachelor Duke died in his sleep at Hardwick. He was succeeded by William Cavendish, Second Earl of Burlington of the second creation, grandson of Lord George Cavendish, the Fifth Duke's brother. This William Cavendish was therefore first cousin once removed of the Bachelor. He married Lady Blanche Howard, daughter of the Earl of Carlisle and Lady Georgiana Cavendish. Blanche was the granddaughter of the Fifth Duke and Georgiana Spencer. It is through Blanche that the present Cavendishes are descended from the famous Georgiana.

With the Bachelor's death came the end of an era for Chatsworth, and a great quiet descended on the house for the next thirty-three years. The new incumbent was a totally different man from the author of the *Handbook*. The Seventh Duke was a scholar, a serious, quiet man, who disliked social life as much as his predecessor enjoyed it. He was a widower for fifty-one years and never ceased to grieve for his dead wife. It is said he never smiled again after she died. One has the feeling he did not smile much before. He was a distinguished mathematician, Second Wrangler and First Smith's Prizeman at Cambridge, Chancellor of London University at the age of twenty-eight, and afterwards Chancellor of Cambridge. He taught his wife geometry on their honeymoon. He was deeply religious, and his way of life was as modest and austere as the man himself.

The Seventh
Duke of
Devonshire
(1808–1891)

The Duke inherited debts which had grown into formidable sums during the long and extravagant reign of his predecessor, and he immediately took steps to reduce the expenditure by getting rid of large numbers of the staff at Chatsworth and his other houses. Then he set to work to recoup the family fortune by planning and financing new enterprises concerned with railways, heavy industry, harbours and docks at Barrow-in-Furness in Lancashire, and building houses, hotels and shops in the seaside resort of Eastbourne in Sussex, where his work as a town planner of the 1870s stands as a memorial to him today.

For a while the ventures at Barrow prospered exceedingly, but like many another before him he backed the same horse too often, and before his plans to spread his interests could come to fruition the industrial businesses declined, in spite of pouring more and more of his own money into them. The failure of the works he had begun and done so much to promote worried and saddened him in his old age.

Paine's Stables

Myself in my sitting room

His sense of duty brought him to Derbyshire to attend to the running of the estate, but the place he loved best was Holker* and he continued to spend most of his time there, in Eastbourne and in London. So the eighteen-sixties, seventies and eighties at Chatsworth passed without incident. Little was added or taken away. It was a twilight time when the blinds of the main rooms were pulled down for months on end.

The Duke's orderly mind caused him to ask Sir James Lacaita to make a catalogue of the library in 1871. It has never been brought up to date, except by notes in the margins, and is still the only catalogue which exists. He bought some books on travel and natural history, including the Audubons, but the most visible sign of his tenure is the church at Edensor with its high spire just taller than the beeches on the hill between the village and the house. Sir Gilbert Scott was responsible for swallowing up the fourteenth-century building, and his rebuilt church was consecrated in 1870.

His home life was enlivened by his four children, Spencer Compton (called Cav), Frederick, Edward and Louisa. The Duke was a most affectionate father. He had been unhappy at Eton himself and did not want his boys to suffer the same fate, so he kept them at home and taught them himself. They all remained the greatest of friends for the rest of their lives, and long after they married they continued to progress together round the country for the annual visits to their father's various houses in special trains.

His only daughter, Louisa, looked after him and her brother Cav (who did not marry for many years) and found herself in charge of the housekeeping of all the houses at the age of fourteen, a task she carried out to the entire satisfaction of everyone concerned. Louisa added to the garden Blanche had made at Hardwick and did a lot of planting at Lismore. When she was thirty she married Admiral Egerton. He joined her family rather than the other way round, and she continued to housekeep for her father. The good-natured Admiral was allowed a writing-table of his own in a recess in the drawing-room at Holker. It was lucky that he was used to making do with a confined space on board ship.

Lord Frederick married Lucy Lyttelton in 1864. He was appointed

*Holker Hall near Cark in Cartmel, Lancashire, which came into the family by marriage in 1756.

Chief Secretary to Ireland in 1882 and was murdered in the Phoenix Park within twelve hours of his arrival in Dublin. Lord and Lady Frederick had no children.

Lord Edward married Emma Lascelles in 1865. She was a remarkably ugly, fat, old woman, with a long upper lip and a protruding lower one. She talked incessantly and sourly about her family and wore a black bonnet in the country and the same bonnet in London with a veil added, and a cape covered in black sequins. She was known in the family as the Slammoth—a mixture between a sloth and a mammoth. They had three sons, Victor, Richard and John. Lord Edward died in 1891 so the eldest son, Victor, eventually became Ninth Duke on the death of his Uncle Cav in 1908.

The Eighth Duke, Spencer Compton (1833–1908)

Harty-Tarty, Uncle Cav, the Duke with the Whiskers, was a politician who served Parliament for half a century, thirty-four years in the House of Commons and sixteen in the House of Lords. Three times he was asked by the Queen to form a government, in 1880, 1886 and 1887, and three times he refused. He held many appointments, including that of Postmaster-General, Chief Secretary for Ireland, Secretary of State for India, Secretary of State for War, and he led the Liberal Party from 1875 until the break with Gladstone's new government over Irish Home Rule in 1886, when he and his followers, the Liberal Unionists, sided with Lord Salisbury's Conservatives. He remained steadfastly opposed to Home Rule for Ireland and because of this he and the Liberal Unionists joined Lord Salisbury's Tory Administration in a coalition from 1892 till 1902. For most of this time he was Lord President of the Council. In 1903, as a Free Trader, he resigned over Tariff Reform. In 1904 he gave up his long-held chairmanship of the Liberal Unionist Association and in 1907, the year before he died, he made his last speech in Parliament.

Because he was immersed in politics he lived mostly in Devonshire House in Piccadilly, but the demands made on nineteenth-century politicians were less exacting than they are now, and there was plenty of time to spend elsewhere.

The Eighth Duke of Devonshire
(1833–1908)

Louise von Alten, wife of the
Eighth Duke (1832–1911)

Uncle Cav did not marry till he was fifty-nine, when the woman to
whom he had been deeply attached for a long time had been a widow for
two years and his own father had been dead a year.

His bride was the Duchess of Manchester, the German-born
Countess Louise von Alten, who had married the Duke of Manchester in
1852 and was the mother of five children. The 'Double Duchess' was
considered a great beauty, though it is hard to recognise it in most of the
likenesses we have of her. The frizzed-up hair and short, thick neck of
her race are the features which strike one, and people I have talked to
who saw her only remember the crazily cracked make-up plastered
thickly over her face, which made a bizarre effect on this *grande dame*
receiving at the top of the staircase at Devonshire House in the days
when only whores painted their faces. But she was old then, and the
claim that 'no one knows how gloriously beautiful a woman can be who
did not see the Duchess of Manchester when she was thirty' is nearly
upheld by the Robert Thorburn portrait of her in about 1853, a blue-
eyed Valkyrie gazing out to sea.

When Louise arrived at Chatsworth there had been no Duchess of
Devonshire for eighty years, and her love of society made a cheerful
impact on the place, from the grand set-piece of a week-long shooting-

35

party to the Christmas treat for the schoolchildren of Edensor, Beeley, Pilsley and Baslow held in the Theatre and still remembered with pleasure by two octogenarians alive today.

She liked playing cards, and winning. But she didn't cash the cheques of friends she knew could not afford the high stakes of the house. There was a set of gambling chips in every room, which made odd companions for the large bibles on special brackets which were already in place to improve the minds of the rare guests of the Seventh Duke.

Uncle Cav is as well described as an Edwardian as his father was a Victorian. He was fond of racing and bridge and tolerated (perhaps even enjoyed) the grossly extravagant entertaining which was the fashion at that time and reached its zenith in the houses where King Edward VII stayed. He and Louise Duchess brought Chatsworth back to life after the long quiet years of his father's time. All the rooms were opened, and huge numbers of people came to stay, usually in the winter for pheasant shooting on a grand scale.

The preparations for the house parties were long and complicated, as the hostesses vied with one another to put on a yet more splendid show, and arranged pleasures and surprises for their guests, who were accustomed to the best of everything.*

Chatsworth had a flying start, not only in its vast size and the number of people it could put up, the grandeur of the big rooms, the pictures, sculptures and the show of plate which could be put on in the dining-room, but also because of the Bachelor Duke's delightful extravagances of orchid and camellia houses, peach houses and vineries, and the crowning glory of Paxton's Great Conservatory, with its tropical forest for a Sunday morning walk.

Mr Herrington, the quiet and charming 'odd man' at Hardwick, who must have been born in his green baize apron, told me that during a party for King Edward and Queen Alexandra the dining-room table was laid early for dinner and 'a man from away' went in, the doors were locked, and he covered the silver candlesticks and ornaments on the table with a secret mixture which made it look frosted. He finished his work just before dinner was ready, and the guests walked arm-in-arm from the Gold Drawing-Room, through the Library and the Dome Room, to

*Some were not impressed. Raymond Asquith wrote from Chatsworth to Katharine Horner in 1906, 'How you would loathe this place. It crushes one by its size and is full of smart shrivelled-up people. There is only one bathroom and that is kept for the King . . .'

be met by the sight of the glittering, frozen silver. When dinner was over the man was locked in again to remove his secret frosty covering, and not till he had finished could the orchids be returned to the greenhouse and the footmen take the silver back to the strong room and lay the table for breakfast.

The pictures, tapestries, furniture and books were taken for granted by the Duke, who had not much interest in them, and added little to them. He inherited none of the passion for collecting so marked in his forebears.

When visiting the English section of the Paris Exhibition with a friend he stopped in front of a superb porphyry table. 'This is splendid,' he said. 'I envy the man who owns this.' His friend glanced at the catalogue to see it was lent from Chatsworth.

Sometimes his friends wanted to go round the State Rooms, so before they arrived he and the Duchess did a dummy run with Mrs Arthur Strong, their librarian. She told them the outstanding facts about the most important objects. On one of these occasions (they had to be repeated because the information, like the guests, did not stay long) Mrs Strong was starting her patter about a famous picture, when the Duchess pointed to a dove hovering over the head of a saint and said in her German accent, 'What is that extrrraordinary bird that's got into the cathedrrral?' Before Mrs Strong could say anything, the Duke mumbled into his beard, 'Oh, my dear, even *I* know that is the Holy Ghost.'

Uncle Cav preferred sleeping to anything else. The tales of his excesses of somnolence are legion, but the one I like best is the Duke of Portland's. 'One afternoon, finding the ministerial bench in the House of Lords occupied, he sat on another bench next to me, and in two minutes he was asleep. When he woke with a start he looked at the clock and said "Good heavens, what a bore, I shan't be in bed for another seven hours."'

He yawned in the middle of his maiden speech in the House of Commons, which so impressed Disraeli that he said, 'He'll do. To anyone who can betray such languor in such circumstances the highest posts should be open.'

He asked the King to dinner at Devonshire House, forgot, and was found asleep in his club by a distracted messenger at dinner-time.

He was to introduce a bill in the House of Lords for the establishment of a new university for London. All the educational authorities among his fellow peers came to hear his speech and there was a full attendance. The Duke never turned up, and the House rose. He had gone to the Turf Club after lunch and fell asleep in the reading-room, never waking till an hour after he was due to speak. At cabinet meetings he rarely said anything, but when pressed for advice the answer was always the same: 'Far better not.'

The Duke hated an exaggerated and affected way of talking. When some orator in the House of Lords ended a flowery speech with, 'This is the proudest day of my life', he murmured to his neighbour,

'The proudest day of *my* life was when my pig won first prize at Skipton Fair.'

An American lady who went into ecstasies over the beauties of Chatsworth was greatly disconcerted when he answered, 'It's a rummy old place.'

The Duke was shabbily dressed, preferring comfort to smartness. He had a fine disregard for honours and orders, specially foreign ones. The Garter was one thing, but when the King of Portugal stayed at Chatsworth and bestowed the Order of the Tower and Sword on him he felt obliged to wear it for dinner and blamed it for the bad hands he was dealt at bridge that evening, saying in front of the Portuguese Minister, 'If I have another poor hand I shall throw this damned Elephant and Castle into the fire.'

It was Louise who liked being surrounded by people, and it was she who invited them to stay. The Duke ambled into meals quite unaware of who was in the house. He once said to Bernard Holland, his biographer, when a house party was assembled before dinner, 'This is all very well but I should like to know who my guests are. Do you know the name of that red-faced man over there?'

His energetic wife planned everything perfectly, but any part of the organisation left to the Duke was invariably forgotten.

He was so bored by having to make a list of who was shooting that having done it once he did not bother to do it again, so when Lord Rosebery, who had not shot the first day, went down to breakfast on the second morning dressed to go out he met his valet in the passage, who said, 'You'd better change your clothes m'lord, you're not on the shooting list.' Lord Rosebery left for London in a rage.

The famous fancy dress ball given at Devonshire House in the year of

The Eighth Duke as the Emperor Charles V
At the Devonshire House Ball, 1897

Louise Duchess as Zenobia, Queen of Palmyra

the Queen's Diamond Jubilee is recorded in a fascinating book of photographs. The stout old Duchess was dressed as Zenobia, Queen of Palmyra—goodness knows why—and she persuaded the Duke to be the Emperor Charles V. There he stands in a flat velvet hat and wrinkled stockings, bored to death and longing to be in bed and asleep.

Uncle Cav died in 1908. Three hundred Members of Parliament of all parties came to his funeral at Edensor to pay their last respects to the revered old Englishman.

The Ninth Duke, his wife, formerly Lady Evelyn Fitzmaurice, and six of their grandchildren, 1934

The Ninth Duke

Victor Christian William (1868–1938)

Victor Christian William Cavendish was the eldest of the three sons of Lord and Lady Edward Cavendish. He was grandson of the Seventh Duke and nephew of the Eighth.

He was elected M.P. for West Derbyshire when he was twenty-three, and the following year he married Lady Evelyn Fitzmaurice, elder daughter of the Fifth Marquess of Lansdowne.

They lived at 37 Park Lane and at Holker Hall in Lancashire and stayed at Chatsworth and Compton Place occasionally with Uncle Cav and Louise. Their characters and tastes were totally different from those of their host and hostess.

Evie abhorred gambling, racing and the lax morals of Edwardian high society. She had been strictly brought up by Lady Lansdowne and was shy of smart people, so could not have enjoyed the sort of company she found at Chatsworth. She and her husband and children led a different kind of life at Holker, centred on the family, house, garden, farm and estate, and his interests in the House of Commons when in London.

The Duke's diaries of the Holker years are a joy to read. He had a droll style of writing which endears him to me. They are full of entries like 'We went to see the new church at Flookborough. Thought it rather askew.' 'Mrs Drewry's funeral. Sad little ceremony. Much warmer. Shot a few rooks after.'

When the Eighth Duke died in 1908 Victor and Evie left Holker to start their life at Chatsworth, which was to last for thirty years. Victor's brother and sister-in-law, Lord Richard and Lady Moyra Cavendish, and their growing family went to the much-loved Holker where, happily, their grandchildren and great-grandchildren live now.

It was some time before the new Duke and Duchess were able to move in to Chatsworth, because it was discovered that the drains, which hardly existed anyway, were in a very poor state, and much work had to be done on them before the big family and huge number of servants which the house required could safely be installed. They lodged at Hardwick while the work was done and constantly travelled the seventeen miles to see how it was getting on.

Victor's diaries of 1908 and 1909 are full of references to Evie 'seeing to the painting' and no doubt many other things at Chatsworth. Drains and painting finished, they moved in early that year, and in August 1909 their youngest child, Anne, was born—the first Cavendish to be born in the house since the eighteenth century.

Victor missed the House of Commons but continued his political career in the Lords. He was deeply interested in agriculture and he loved the country and the people who were close to the land. He liked shooting and cricket, he played golf on his private course in the park and carried out the inescapable duties of a large landowner with quiet enjoyment. Such engagements meant endless travel between London, Sussex, County Waterford, Yorkshire and Derbyshire. Things sometimes went awry. My favourite entry in his diary, headed 'London', reads, 'Important meeting in Buxton. Missed train. Rather glad.'

The Duke's great love was his Shire horses. He built a splendid range of stables for them in Pilsley and was in at the birth of the foals whenever he was at Chatsworth, even if it meant getting up in the middle of the night. He brought his best animals with him from Holker, and also his Shorthorns, which were kept at the Home Farm at Barbrook in the park. There are many references to the Shires in his diary: 'Premier is getting very vicious. Went for the man last night. Hope there will be no accident.' 'Tremendous thunderstorm. Mother Hubbard dropped dead.' And of a cow, 'Butterfly cast her calf. Very troublesome.'

The Devonshires also had business matters to attend to. On the death of the Eighth Duke over half a million pounds had to be raised to pay death duty. Added to the substantial 'running debt' left by the failure of the Seventh Duke's business ventures it forced some major sales. In 1912 Victor and Evie decided to part with the twenty-five books printed by William Caxton (1422–1491) and the 1,347 volumes of plays which the Bachelor Duke bought from Sarah Siddons' brother, John Kemble (1757–1823). These included the first four Shakespeare folios and thirty-nine Shakespeare quartos. They were sold to the Huntington Library in California.

It was understandable that they wanted to be rid of the distasteful business of owing huge sums of money, and I suppose that is why they decided on the neat deal of these precious books; so off they went, bang, like swotting a fly. But it left an irreparable gap in the library.

During and immediately after the Great War a large acreage of land was sold in Somerset, Sussex and Derbyshire, followed by Devonshire House in London. Devonshire House, its stables, coach-house and garden occupied a site of about three acres in Piccadilly facing south over Green Park and bounded by Stratton Street, the Lansdowne Passage and Berkeley Street. There were two lawn tennis courts in the garden, and tennis parties were the thing for the Aunts.

The Duke was Civil Lord of the Admiralty in 1915–16, and in 1916 he went to Canada as Governor-General and Commander-in-Chief, taking his wife and six younger children with him.

The move to 2 Carlton Gardens took place in 1920. Evie came home to oversee what must have been a dismal as well as a mammoth task.

Carlton Gardens was one of those grand London houses designed for entertaining and showing furniture and pictures with no regard to the comfort of its inhabitants. There were so few bedrooms that the butler slept in a sort of cupboard on the stairs, and Andrew had a camp bed in his mother's sitting-room.

After all these sales were completed they settled down to the old routine and lived in just the same way as before the Great War, with much the same number of people to look after the houses (though the gardeners at Chatsworth were reduced to forty instead of nearly eighty). There were still few labour-saving devices, and the staff was not idle. And so it was in many houses of the same kind, contrary to the general belief of young people now that such a way of life ended with the Great War.

While her husband attended to the out-of-doors, Evie was absorbed by the collections, and got to know a great deal about them. Her interest ranged from the general to the particular, and when she was an old woman living at Hardwick (a round peg in a round hole if ever there was one) she was apt to pin you before a tapestry and would lecture for hours on a tiny piece of it, explaining how the shape of a shoe, or a leaf, or the horn of an animal, proved something or other.

She sought the company of museum curators. If she had had to earn her living she would have been happy in such a job herself and was delighted when, at work on her favourite task of mending tapestry, she was watched by an expert on the subject, who told her she was wasting her time being a duchess and should go and work for him.

She was a great restorer and preserver and the pristine state of many of the things in the house is due to the care she took of them. A perfectionist, she once sacked a housekeeper for half glazing some chintz instead of going the whole hog. Such a nicety would be lost on people nowadays, but it was the kind of detail she really cared about.

Her sensitive nose could smell dry rot a mile away, and she waged a private war against woodworm. Her plan was to give them concussion, and for this purpose she kept a little hammer in her bag to bang the furniture where they lurked.

Evie was careful to the point of meanness over small things, and she could not bear waste of any kind, There is a story, told me by one of the Aunts, of her sticking a three-halfpenny stamp on an envelope with the wrong address on it. She rang for a footman. He appeared after two or three minutes and she asked for a kettle of boiling water. The footman went to the kitchen and a kettle was put on. In due course he made the long journey back to the drawing-room, and she solemnly supervised steaming the three-halfpenny stamp off the envelope. During the last war she used to give a pudding at lunch which was made of the barley the barley-water had been made of. The enormous green cut velvet bed at Hardwick was thought to be extravagant on sheets, so a guest given that magnificent room slept on a camp bed at its foot.

Sharp of feature, small of eye, preferring inanimate objects to humans, she saw mistakes everywhere and was ever critical of her family and her servants. I never heard her praise anyone. Once I was grumbling about something I thought had been badly done at Chatsworth, when Obbie St Albans, her brother-in-law who knew her well, said, 'Take care you don't get like your grandmother-in-law, *an unpleasant woman accustomed to authority*.' But she was kind to me, I think because she liked my children.

She was not in the least interested in human comfort, but was very aware of her responsibility for the well-being of the works of art in her care. My mother-in-law told me that one day Granny Evie opened a box of Raphael drawings, piled them carefully on top of each other on the table, put them back in their box, and, as she snapped the fastener, said, 'There! They've been aired for this year.'

The biggest structural change she made at Chatsworth was the alteration of the staircase in the Painted Hall and the ceiling and doorways and cornice of the Oak Stairs. There was much talk of pulling down the Bachelor Duke's long wing and Belvedere Tower above the Theatre, but it never got further than talk.

The family never stayed long in one place. The year was punctuated by moves which were determined by politics and sport and the need for the conscientious proprietor to pay an annual visit to his estates. November, December and January were spent at Chatsworth, then Lismore Castle for February, March and April; to London for May, June and most of July; a short visit to Chatsworth to include Bakewell Show before Bolton Abbey for grouse shooting in August and half of September; Hardwick for the partridges in October and back to Chatsworth again. Compton Place was let.

'So when did you go to Chiswick?' I asked Granny.

'Chiswick? Oh, we sometimes used it for breakfast.'

When they came back to England in 1921 after five years in Canada the changes wrought by war were as evident at Chatsworth as anywhere else. The most noticeable was the demolition of Paxton's and Decimus Burton's Great Conservatory. It was a tragedy, but there seemed to be no alternative. The tropical garden it contained needed ten men to look after it and immense quantities of coal to heat it. Neither men nor coal

The Painted Hall during alterations to the stairs and galleries, 1911

Evelyn Duchess, Mistress of the Robes to Queen Mary, at the Coronation of King George VI, 1937. Her page was her grandson, Michael Baillie.

were available during the war, so all the plants were dead, and the place was desolate.

The decision was made to knock it down, but so sound was the structure that this proved impossible, and it had to be blown up. One explosion was not enough and just broke the glass, splinters of which still litter the garden. Repeated blastings took place till only the stone foundations remained, and the Great Conservatory was no more. The pride and joy of the Bachelor Duke's garden existed for only eighty years.

The Devonshires did not go to Ireland during the Troubles, and although Lismore Castle escaped being burnt down, it was occupied by both sides during the Civil War, and enough damage was done to the roof and to many of the rooms to make it uninhabitable. When it was considered to be safe for the family to return they stayed in the hotel in the town, and there, on Easter Sunday 1925, the Duke suffered a stroke which cruelly affected him until his death thirteen years later. His brain was damaged, and his nature changed from being the most easygoing, good-humoured man imaginable to an irritable old gentleman who laid about him with his stick, whacking fellow-members of his club,

The Ninth Duke and seventeen grandchildren, Christmas 1931. Billy Hartington is the tallest boy, Arbell Mackintosh comes next, then Andrew Cavendish and Maurice Macmillan.

stationmasters, footmen and anyone else who came within range. People learned to be nimble in his presence. But he kept his love for babies and little children up to the age of five, and was never happier than with his younger grandchildren.

The Duke's affliction cast a gloom over family life, and those years of his decline must have been a great strain on Evie, who nobly kept up a pretence that everything was normal.

He was still able to get about the estate, and his companion was usually John Maclauchlan. Maclauchlan reigned as head keeper from 1905 till 1950. He was a legendary figure, tall and authoritative, and all the more so since he had the ear of the Duke. He lived in a big house with a Paxtonian tower, and had a chauffeur. When we moved to Edensor in 1947 he sent for me (no question of him coming to our house). I was received very formally, shown into the parlour by his daughter and asked to sit down. The great man entered and said with all the authority of the ruler of a huge domain, 'Lady Hartington, I've sent for you to tell you you can go wherever you

A 'Stink Hog', with chauffeur Bill Hawes, and footman, *c.*
1913

John
Maclauchlan

like.' He was not only in charge of the shooting, but he was made farm manager and so was responsible for the beloved Shires. Shooting and the horses were Victor's great interests to the end of his life.

The two men tooled round the country in the back of a huge brown Rolls-Royce (not that the Duke ever referred to it as such, but ordered the 'Stink Hog' to be brought round). It was driven by Mr Burdekin, the Duke's chauffeur, whose instructions were never to exceed twenty-five miles an hour. On the rare occasions when he went a little faster the Duke used to bang on the glass partition with his stick and shout, 'Burdekin, Burdekin, what d'you think you are, a crazy cow with a tin tied on its tail?'

As in the Eighth Duke's years the winter shooting parties and Christmas were the busiest times at Chatsworth. Every November the Duke and Duchess of Portland came over from Welbeck for four or five days' pheasant shooting. Maclauchlan called the Duke of Portland 'His Other Grace'.

Although the two duchesses were friends there was some rivalry between them over their houses and the things in them. For these parties a great display of gold and silver was put on in the dining-room. Winnie Portland, well aware that every piece was out on show, used to tease Evie Devonshire by waiting for a pause in the conversation and saying, 'Evie, will you take us down to the strong room after dinner and show us the plate?'

King George V and Queen Mary came to stay at Chatsworth in 1933 for the Royal Show when it was held at Derby. Sir Roland Burke, the head agent, was honorary director, and more or less ran the Royal from the Estate Office at Chatsworth. In those days the show was held at a different place each year, and when it was at Newcastle the sleeper train bringing passengers from London stayed in a siding till it was a reasonable time to get up. Two farmers walking down the platform saw the recumbent figure of Victor, sound asleep in true Cavendish fashion, his pink head on the pillow. 'That's a fine Large White,' one said. 'That's no Large White. That's the Duke of Devonshire,' answered his companion, a Derbyshire man no doubt, who could tell the difference.

To go back to the house: In 1937 someone noticed that the ceiling of the Painted Hall was beginning to sag. It was discovered that the middle was nine inches out of true and was on the point of collapsing on to the marble floor twenty-nine feet below.

It did not occur to Granny to send for an 'expert' from London. She had complete confidence in Mr Shimwell, who was in charge, and he knew that Bill Maltby, Arthur Hicks and the other men had the skill to restore what is probably the most important room in the house as part of their everyday work. That is the strength of Chatsworth. The people on the spot are perfectly capable of doing the most highly skilled and difficult jobs, and they would be greatly surprised if anyone doubted their competence. The only 'outsider' to be called in was Mr Constantine, technical assistant of the Sheffield City Art Gallery, who repainted the cracks lying on his back in a sort of barber's chair specially made by Maltby.

The joiners took up the floors of the rooms above so that plasterers could get to work, and Arthur Hicks (b. 1906), master plasterer, was the man who actually carried out the long and tedious task of giant's dentistry which pulled the ceiling back from disaster. It took them two years, a few feet at a time, and in the summers the tourists had to weave their way through the scaffolding below.

The ceiling, painted by Laguerre in 1692–4, measures sixty-four feet by twenty-six. Mr Hicks described to me how the joiners propped up the whole ceiling, held by boards with soft packing, and braced it up to its original position. The ceiling was suspended from the bearers of the floor above. These were affected by death-watch beetle, and small steel girders were fitted to replace some of the old oak timbers, jointed with wooden pegs. It was a laborious and painstaking job, but eventually the structural part was made sound. Then came the moment of reckoning: what would be the state of the painted plaster when uncovered? It was expected that due to the bracing-up operation there would be cracks, and Mr Hicks recalled how 'There were more than we thought, and some big holes too.' It looked like a jigsaw puzzle. The ceiling was uncovered six feet at a time. Every crack and hole had to be chipped out. Hicks did this with an old army pocket-knife, sharpened every morning, and wore out three of them in the course of the job.

Each crack was primed with 'fancy spirits, which we were warned not to drink' to prevent discolouring the painting, and then refilled with plaster, which had to be squeezed into the riven laths to make the key to hold it up. When firmly set the patches were primed by Vic Fewkes and Jack Bedford, the house painters, ready for Mr Constantine, who repainted the now missing parts of the picture.

When it was finished Jack Bedford said to Hicks, 'Well, lad, thou'll always be remembered. I shan't tell thee where thou art, but I've put thy initials and Victor's [the other painter's] and mine. So we be always there on the ceiling.'

Granny watched the progress of this work with great interest. Hicks told me, 'Her Grace used to stand on the catwalk, which was the nearest she could get to the work. She came on one occasion when the artist was painting Hercules' face. She said, "Oh Mr Constantine, haven't you made his nose very pugilistic?" So with two strokes of the brush he completely altered the face, and Her Grace was very satisfied. And you should have seen when that dirt came off—we found a whole donkey you couldn't see before.'

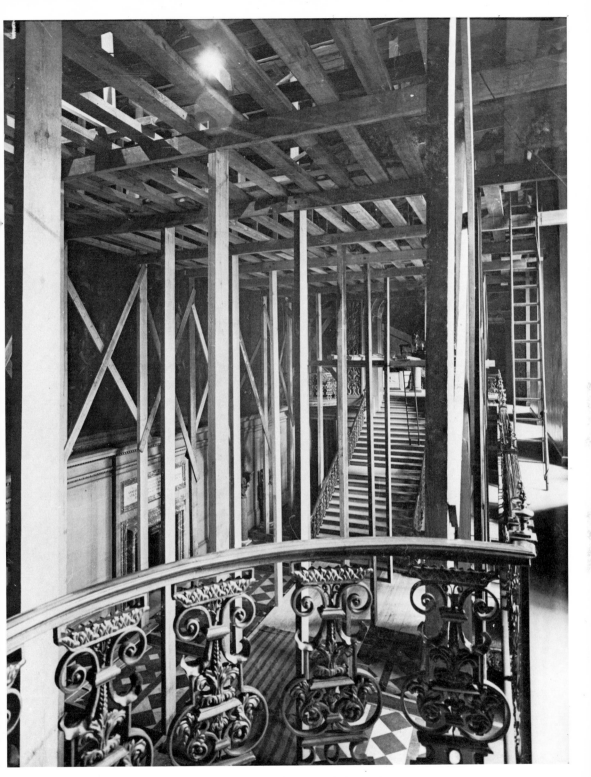

The Painted Hall when the ceiling was being mended, 1936

The Household in the Twenties and Thirties

A great number of people was needed to make the house work, and the organisation was rather like that of a ship, self-contained and having an accepted chain of command which, like the wages, had changed little for a hundred years.

The Comptroller

The head of all the Cavendish households was the comptroller. Until the Great War he was a remote and exalted figure who worked at Devonshire House and was seldom seen in the country. When Victor and Evie came back from Canada the comptroller was Mr Shimwell (1895–1980), and he held that post from 1921 till 1950. After that he was clerk of works for the estate and was in charge of the alterations to the house in 1958 and 1959. He retired in 1964. I often feel I should not be sitting in this room today had it not been for Willie Shimwell. He was one of the cleverest men I have ever met.

He started doing odd jobs at Chatsworth at Christmas 1907, and left school to be on the regular payroll in 1908 when he was twelve and a half. Shimwell's first job in the house was bell-boy. He sat by the bell-board and when one of the guests rang for his valet the name of the room registered on the board, and he had to run and find the valet to tell him he was needed by his gentleman. He also ran the three-quarters of a mile to Edensor with telegrams before a telephone was installed in the house. He acted as caddy for any of the guests who played golf, along with other boys at Edensor School who were detailed for the job by the agent, much to the annoyance of the schoolmaster, Mr Wragg (father of Tom Wragg, librarian from 1964 to 1978). Shimwell did a spell as a postillion at Devonshire House, and then went into the Estate Office at Chatsworth as a clerk. His outstanding ability was soon recognised, and in 1916 the

Willie and Maud Shimwell at
Sto's coming of age party, 1965

Duke and Duchess sent for him to go to Canada to help to run their household staff at Government House, Ottawa. So successful was he that when they came home in 1921 he was appointed comptroller of Chatsworth and 2 Carlton Gardens at the age of twenty-six. For some years he was also the Duke's private secretary. He travelled with the family to Bolton Abbey and Lismore, and was the great friend and confidant of the grandchildren in the twenties and thirties. Granny relied on him for everything to do with the houses and their inhabitants, added to which he ran the Home Farm for her.

The comptroller was over all the Chatsworth staff except the librarian and the Duchess's private secretary, with both of whom he worked closely. He looked after the fabric of the house, the stables and the important buildings in the garden, the cascade, the fountains and other waterworks, the lakes and conduits on the moor above the house which are reservoirs for these, the private roads and lodges in the park, security and everything to do with the opening of the house and garden to the public, engaging and arranging the rota of wardens, ticket sellers and car parkers, and he resolved the thousand and one problems which arose from a houseful of people whose work forced them to live in close proximity with others not of their choosing. He organised the charity events in the house and the park, and arranged the Christmas parties for the schoolchildren of Baslow, Beeley, Pilsley and Edensor. In his office was an assistant comptroller, who paid the wages and did the accounts, and a clerk.

Shimwell told me how the house was run, and since he died in 1980 I have talked to other people who were part of the indoor staff in the twenties and thirties who still live in estate houses within two miles of Chatsworth. Their recollections of their work and the order of their lives are so impossible to believe in the 1980s that I have asked their permission to record what they have told me. It is reassuring to meet these smart ladies and hear them talking and laughing about the way of life here fifty years ago, taken for granted by them then and remembered with amused and affectionate tolerance half a century later.

The Staff

The head man in the house was the butler. Then came the Duke's valet, the under butler, the groom of the chambers, two footmen, stewards' room footman, housekeeper, the Duchess's maid, head housemaid, two second housemaids, two third housemaids, two fourth housemaids, two fifth housemaids and two sixth housemaids, two sewing women, cook, first kitchen maid, second kitchen maid, vegetable maid, two or three scullery maids, two stillroom maids, dairy maid, six laundry maids and the Duchess's secretary. All these people lived in the house. The odd man, upholsterer, sculleryman, two scrubbing women, laundry porter, steam boiler man, coal man, two porter's lodge attendants, two night firemen, night porter and two window cleaners came daily. So did the joiners, plumbers and electricians.

The groom of the chambers was responsible for the writing-tables. There was a properly equipped writing-table in every bedroom as well as in the drawing-rooms, study, etc. This job fell to the footmen when the groom of the chambers left and was not replaced in the early thirties.

The under butler was in charge of the silver and all the other plate and was told by the cook what dishes she wanted for the dining-room meals.

He sat at the head of the table in the servants' hall and did the carving. On his right sat the head housemaid with her ten assistants in order of precedence, on his left the first footman and so on down the scale. Their food was brought from the kitchen by the odd man who also washed up for the servants' hall.

The Duke's valet was his personal servant who called him in the morning, looked after his clothes, packed and unpacked and travelled with him. He was directly responsible to the Duke and so had a privileged position.

Henry Bennett, who was footman from 1928 to 1934, recalls the footmen's jobs at that time:

In 1928 I applied for the situation as a footman to Their Graces, the Duke and Duchess of Devonshire, at Chatsworth. I was invited to an interview at 2 Carlton Gardens by Her Grace, who at first thought I was not tall enough, as the footman I was to replace was six foot two inches, and was nicknamed 'Long Henry', myself being only five foot nine inches, but after some consideration I was thought suitable.

On arrival at Chatsworth, so aptly named 'The Palace of the Peak', I was asked if I would take the name of Henry: the previous footman had that name, and the Stewards' Room footman was Ernest, and that being mine it would make things easier all round, so I adopted the name Henry. My salary, to commence, was to be £42 per year, with liveries, one semi-state and a black suit yearly, and a black mackintosh, and a white coat and cap for car work in London when Her Grace was delivering cards, which were turned down at the corners to let people know she had called in person. The semi-state livery meant we had to breech when over six for dinner, and we were supplied with black pumps, with a buckle on, which were uncomfortable to start with. The state livery was kept in London.

The Footmen's Room on the ground floor had large cupboards to house our liveries, two armchairs, and a large table for pressing clothes, and here we cleaned the shoes; and my first Christmas at midnight I prepared to clean thirty-six pairs of various shoes, ladies' and gentlemen's. If the gentlemen did not travel with a valet we had to do the valeting. Outside the room was a large bell-board, which, when the bells rang, we could not fail to hear and see which one had registered.

The male staff slept in the East Attic bedrooms; all beds were feather ones, ideal for the cold winter nights. There were also fireplaces in most bedrooms, an armchair, chest of drawers, and in some, wardrobes. The bathroom and toilet, in one, was situated at the end of the long passage. Pictures of bygone days adorned the bedroom and passage walls.

Our duties were to lay the tables for breakfast and teas, but for luncheon and dinner we helped to lay under the jurisdiction of the under butler. Unless there was a very big party the Duke and Duchess and their guests helped themselves to breakfast and teas, but we always waited at luncheon and dinner.

We were always pleased when we could get away from the head servants. Then we could relax, talk freely and enjoy a good laugh, quoting the day when the steward's room footman broke the cover of the soup tureen. He had to report it to the housekeeper who said, 'What do you want, boy?' He replied, 'I regret, Madam, the summit of the soup tureen has lost its equilibrium with disastrous results.' This was greeted with peals of laughter.

The cleaning of writing-table silver was our responsibility, and our duty was to see that all the tables were laid out properly with the Chatsworth paper and the pens straight on the pen trays, the water bottles with brush for wetting the stamps, the glass bowl with wet sponge for cleaning the pen nibs (as fountain pens were not so much used in those days). Every day we washed the silver used at the four meals and all the glass in the large wooden sinks in the Under Butler's Pantry. The china from breakfast and tea was washed up in the Still Room, and plates and vegetable dishes from lunch and dinner were attended to by the daily women. The carrying of meals was on butler's trays by the 'odd men' and footmen, the system being their duty every other day, but for big dinners men from the estate helped us out.

During the winter when parties were held, a number of fires had to be attended to, this meant fifteen each time; as they needed attention four times daily this meant a grand total of sixty for a day. This chore we did every other day, each took a bucket of coal, luckily the coalman had them placed in convenient cupboards. The shutting up of rooms took a considerable time, but we did this together; it meant blinds, shutters and curtains, taking half an hour each person. Also, we had to ensure all doors to the house from the grounds and front entrance were locked at the different times during the year.

Shooting parties were a grand affair; usually lunch was taken out to various places. Lord Hartington's butler and one footman were detailed to do it. Tea was prepared in the Gold Drawing-Room on round tables. Her Grace officiated at one table to pour the tea, and some other lady at various tables when the number was a large one. The gong sounded in the Painted Hall for dressing three-quarters of an hour before dinner. The guests assembled in the Gold Drawing-Room, and when the butler announced dinner the gentlemen, with a lady guest, linked arms and walked through the long Library and Ante-Library, to the Dining-Room. The table was laid with ornate pieces of silver, like silver pilgrim bottles and six silver vases adorned with eagles, filled with exquisite orchids from the greenhouses, which were nightly admired by the guests and left a lasting impression on all. The menu consisted mostly of four courses with dessert, coffee and appropriate wines and liqueurs. On Sundays, if there was a shooting party, the table was laid with gilt decorations, and in the centre a large, oval gilt container filled with fruit, sometimes cantaloup melons and grapes grown in the greenhouses; rather like a harvest festival, with so much fruit displayed.

Henry Bennett, Sally Jones (in front of him)
and a group of housemaids, c. 1930

Henry Bennett in semi-state livery, 1928

All the family came for Christmas, so it was always a large party. With so many grandchildren—twenty, I believe, at this time—it meant six nurseries with six nannies and six nursery-maids who were responsible for cooking breakfast, porridge and toast, but the Steward's Room footman was detailed to carry all the nursery food from the kitchen, which was certainly a difficult undertaking with such a large house party, as it meant a large number of people for meals. On Christmas Day quite a number of children came to the Dining-Room for lunch, some having to sit on cushions to reach the table.

The tall Christmas tree was gaily decorated in the Painted Hall, with a cheerful log fire burning in the fireplace. The presents were given out to the staff by Their Graces and members of their family. The footmen for several years received six pairs of black socks, which were useful and always meant you were suitably dressed with your livery and black shoes. One year I was given a black and white scarf.

Christmas tea was laid on round tables in the Gold Drawing-Room, and except for babies in arms, all came for tea; there was always a grand spread of Christmas cakes. One year the Hunting Tower was depicted and cakes in the shape of yule logs, all made by the different stillroom maids, and of course an abundance of crackers. Babies in arms, carried by their devoted nannies, arrived in time to see the tree light up. The outdoor activities meant some guests would be late for lunch, so hot food was left in the dishes and placed in the large steel fenders in front of the fires to keep hot—no heated trolleys in those days.

If the House was only occupied with Their Graces and Miss Saunders we were allowed off duty every other day, from after lunch. We were lucky in being able to play golf; some played football and cricket in season, otherwise tennis. In the winter we always had snow, so we indulged in tobogganing. We enjoyed dances at the Institute, which it was then called, and visited the neighbouring villages for whist drives and dances. If we became bored we did numerous jigsaw puzzles, and we had quite a craze for making woollen rugs.

When we moved to Bolton Abbey or Hardwick there was no electric light; oil lamps and candles were the order. A man was kept to see that the lamps contained oil, wicks trimmed and lamp glasses cleaned. It was the footmen's duty to put the lamps around the house. His Grace invariably liked candles, so quite a number of lighted candles adorned his study. When the ladies had retired late at night, the footmen had to extinguish the lamps, and place electric torches, silver candlesticks and matches outside the Drawing-Room for the guests to pick up and light themselves to their rooms, the order being that the last gentleman to leave the Drawing-Room saw that all lamps left there were extinguished. It proved so popular, and allowed us to retire earlier, that this plan was adopted at Chatsworth.

I enjoyed my seven years' service at Chatsworth, and over the years have benefited from the knowledge and experience gained there.

After the Great War the footmen still powdered their hair when there was a party, but this practice stopped in 1924. They wore full livery if there were more than six for dinner till 1938: lemon coats, dark blue breeches and white stockings.

The Stewards' Room footman (who also wore livery) waited on Mr Shimwell and the head servants, the Duke's valet, the Duchess's maid and visiting valets and ladies' maids who ate in the Stewards' Room.

The housekeeper was equal to the butler and was over all the female servants except the kitchen staff. She sat opposite the butler at meals. The Duchess's maid was the female equivalent to the Duke's valet and was directly responsible to the Duchess. Her varied duties ranged from dressmaking (Granny's maid, Miss Webb, had been at Worth and so was very good with her needle), copying and altering clothes and even hats, mending tapestries and needlework, to cleaning the Duchess's clothes with petrol. This was done in the Orangery so the fumes could escape. I remember her digging her toes in when asked by Granny to milk a goat during the war. The goat turned out to be a male, so her good sense prevailed.

The dairy maid received the milk and eggs from the farm and was responsible for issuing both to the kitchen and stillroom and milk to the housemaids' room, laundry maids and servants' hall. She pickled the eggs, made the butter and helped the stillroom maids at busy times, and cooked for the Duke when he stayed at Chatsworth alone and the Duchess and the rest of the household were elsewhere.

The coal man, who was very strong, was capable of carrying a whisket weighing a hundredweight up eighty stairs to the nursery and to various bunkers all round the house. He collected the ashes from the housemaids' boxes and put them in a wagon which stood by the back door whence they were hauled to the ash tip a mile away in the park.

The housemaids fetched their breakfast, tea and supper from the kitchen to eat in their own room and had lunch in the servant's hall. When there was a party they started work at five in the morning and were called by the night watchman on his final round. The first job was to clean the steel grates that had contained coal fires. The footmen were supposed to rake them out last thing at night (usually in the early hours of the morning as they had to wait until the Duke and his guests had gone to bed). Even so the steel bars were often hot. The housemaids cleaned them with a burnisher made of chain on leather which was worked with rhythm to produce shine with no scratches. They started by loosening the grime on the steel bars with spittle or brasso and then worked with three different types of emery paper, coarse, medium and fine, the coarse for the bars, which had taken the most heat and were the hardest to clean, the medium and fine for polishing the sheet steel before burnishing. The knobs were taken off to be polished and finished with a burnisher, and finally the firedogs and the fender were done. It took up to two hours to do this. They swept the carpets and used tea-leaves or wet paper to absorb the dust. The upper housemaids followed with the dusting. Everything had to be ready by eight a.m. and the blinds were pulled down as soon as the rooms were cleaned to prevent the light reaching the books and paintings. Mr Thompson, the librarian, was strict about this. The housemaids went into the dining-room just before dinner and swept the carpet with long-handled brushes so the pile all lay in the same direction.

Gladys Hopkins applied through Mrs Johnson's agency of Wolverhampton for the job of equal fifth housemaid in 1925. There were nineteen other applicants. She was not interviewed but was engaged on the strength of her references from her former employer, Lady Stamford, her handwriting and the composition of her letter. Her wages were £24 a year plus £6 10s a year beer money and 4s a week laundry money. She left after three years to earn £46 at Lady Harcourt's. Luckily for Chatsworth she had fallen in love with Jesse Grafton, and when Miss Saunders, the Duchess's secretary, asked her to come back as equal third housemaid at a wage of £36 she decided Jesse was worth losing £10 a year. He is still one of the key men in the house, and, he and Mrs Grafton live close by at Beeley.

Sally Jones came in 1929 through Mrs Hunt's London agency. She had been at Chirk Castle for three years. (If a girl placed by Mrs Hunt stayed three years she received a pair of kid gloves from the agency.) She was nineteen, but said she was twenty-one. Her wages as equal fourth housemaid were £30 a year plus £6 10s a year beer money and 4s a week laundry money. Sally worked at Chatsworth till 1936 when she married Len Barnes, Andrew's driver for many years. They were not allowed to meet when in the house or during the day, so when they were courting she used to lean out of the window to wave to him.

Chatsworth had a reputation for poor wages. There were no rises, and the under-servants did not stay long till the housekeeper started monthly dances in the theatre where they could invite their boy-friends. The housemaids were supposed to have one afternoon a week and every other evening off, but there was usually too much work for this, and they had very little free time. They had to be in by nine-thirty in the winter and ten o'clock in the summer.

When tea was substituted for beer, cash was paid in lieu, hence the 'beer money' in addition to the wages. In 1931 income tax rose to 5s in the pound under Ramsay MacDonald, and Granny decided on stringent economies and stopped the beer money. As it was a considerable part of the wages and was in the contract of employment it rankled terribly, and no wonder.

The housemaids had to buy their own uniforms: print dresses for morning, black with little white aprons for the afternoon and black for the evening, and white organdie caps which were fastened with elastic at the back. They made these themselves.

For the upper housemaids, besides all the ordinary work, there was 'maiding' to do. They looked after the lady guests in the bedrooms allocated to them for cleaning, unpacked for them when they arrived, called them in the morning, pressed their clothes, ran the bath, squeezed

Seven housemaids, Sally Jones in the middle of the front row, *c.* 1930

the toothpaste on to the toothbrush, turned the stockings to slip the feet into and laid an evening dress and clean underclothes on the bed before dinner. Hot water was carried to the bedrooms in brass cans placed in the china bowl on the washstand with a clean and folded linen towel under the handle. This was done four times a day before meals and the slops taken away afterwards in white china slop pails. The coal fires in the bedrooms were lit about four p.m. so that it was reasonably warm when it was time to dress for dinner. The last round of the bedrooms was made at ten p.m. with the hot-water bottles, the fires were made up and the final can of hot water put on the wash-stand.

The blankets were covered with cream coloured jap silk spreads made by Mary Ball, one of the sewing women. She also made 'eiderdowns' of quilted jap silk stuffed with cotton wool. All the beds were made by the head and second housemaids, and the mattresses were turned every day. The massive bed now in the Leicester bedroom had the biggest and heaviest and Gladys had to kneel on the middle of the mattress to get enough purchase to roll it into position for turning. The housemaids' own beds had feather mattresses on wool or hair mattresses on wooden slats. They slept two or three in a bedroom and moved bedrooms as they became more senior in their jobs.

I asked Sally Barnes why the housemaids all came from away and local girls were not considered. 'Oh, *talk*,' she said, 'tittle-tattle. They never had local people in the front of the house.'

The Laundry

The laundry maids were a law unto themselves and had more freedom than the housemaids. There were six of them. They cooked for themselves and ate in the laundry and only went to the servant's hall on Christmas Day. They had a bath in a wooden tub (half a beer barrel, Mrs Bond told me) on Saturday nights. The head was first to get in, followed by her five helpers in order of seniority. More hot water was tipped in as the bathing progressed. Imagine the horrible grey soapy puddle the last one must have got into.

Chatsworth laundry did the washing for Devonshire House (2 Carlton Gardens after 1920), Hardwick and Bolton Abbey, so there was never a slack time. The laundry porter, helped by the maids, carried up the heavy baskets of linen when they were delivered at the lodge from the station. The steam boiler attendant looked after the laundry machinery which was driven by water power from the same source as the Emperor Fountain. His boiler heated the water for use in the laundry, the steel hot table in the kitchen, a drying rack in the brushing room and a hot cupboard for plates near the entrance to the Great Dining-Room.

The head laundry maid used to go to see the housekeeper on Monday mornings. Except for that interview she arranged her work and that of her girls herself. She was a much respected member of the household, very proud of her department and quick to return a badly folded or ironed item to the girls to be done again. Some of the tablecloths were fourteen yards long and took four people to fold them. The Bolton Abbey napkins were (and still are) a yard square, and it was a terrible job to get them clean if red wine was spilt on them. Irons of several different sizes were heated on the fire, and the large ones, weighing fourteen pounds, gave a gloss to the damask. Marjorie Watt, now Mrs Bond, was laundry maid from 1924 till she married in 1930. She lives in Pilsley now and wrote the following account of a week in the laundry in the 1920s:

Four laundrymaids,
Marjorie Watt front
right, *c*. 1926

The week had began for us on *Friday*. Hampers which arrived on Thursday
night had to be sorted for washing that day.

Saturday. Dry sheets in drying cupboard and fold.

Sunday. Had to go to church. Sat in back row. Clean own room.

Monday. Up at 5 a.m. to mangle sheets ready for ironing. After breakfast
wash personal items, in my case for Lady Anne, Lord Charles and Miss
Saunders. In the afternoon started ironing, went on till 7 or 8 o'clock.

Tuesday. Iron all day.

Wednesday. Iron all day, including personal items.

Thursday. Pack up hampers and personal items for the various destinations
after having been examined by head laundry maid. Clean tables and airing
rooms for next week.

Marjorie's wages were £30 a year plus 18*s* a week board wages and no
beer money. She had one week and one weekend holiday during the
year.

The Kitchen

Mrs Tanner was cook at Chatsworth from November 1924. She had
been with Lord and Lady Savile as first kitchen maid. Lord Savile
wanted his cook to have lessons with Escoffier in the Hotel Cecil in

London but the cook was not interested, so Mrs Tanner took the chance to go in her place. The lessons cost three guineas each. When she was at the Saviles' villa in the south of France she went into the kitchens of the Hôtel de Paris in Monte Carlo and other famous restaurants, and Lord Savile paid the chefs for this privilege with golden louis, and so she learned her trade. She was a famous cook.

Her daughter Maud (who later married Willy Shimwell, the Comptroller) started in the Chatsworth kitchen as vegetable maid in 1926 when her wages were 18s a week plus 2s 6d beer money. Maud became first kitchen maid to her mother and eventually cook. She lives next to Mrs Barnes in Edensor now.

The first kitchen maid cooked for the school room and nursery, and the second kitchen maid cooked for the servants. The vegetable maid did the vegetables for the family. She did her own washing up. The scullery maids did the vegetables for the servants and washed up for the cook and kitchen maids. Maud got up at six, cleaned the cook's sitting-room and took her a cup of tea. Then she laid the cook's table, set out all the knives and the other utensils in order, and saw that everything was at hand. She chopped parsley and prepared other garnishes and then started on the vegetables. She worked till after lunch and had from two to five p.m. off. One girl was left on duty in the afternoons to watch the stock-pots.

At this time there were six in the kitchen and they ate in the kitchen maids' sitting-room. They had a man to clean the coppers. The cooking was done on gas which was made at the gas yard near the kitchen garden till December 1939 when the house was connected to the main. One of the stoves was specially low for the big copper stock-pots which were too heavy to lift and had taps at the bottom to strain off the stock.

Granny heard that the kitchen maids had never seen the drawing-rooms, so she took them on a prolonged tour. 'We were properly educated that day,' Maud Shimwell told me.

The housemaids and kitchen maids were not allowed to speak to each other, but this rule only obtained at Chatsworth, so they looked forward to the visits to Lismore and Bolton Abbey where they could make friends without hindrance.

The only time the housemaids saw the kitchen was on the day of the annual staff party when they were asked by Mrs Tanner to give a hand. 'We filled the vol-au-vent cases and bridge rolls, cut up the fruit salad and that sort of thing,' Sally Barnes told me.

Stillroom maid, Dorothy Cunnington (right) with Lady Dorothy Macmillan at Sto's wedding, 1967

The Stillroom

Dorothy Cunnington came in 1930 as the head stillroom maid and stayed till she married Sidney Child in 1939. She had one full-time helper, and the dairy maid went to the stillroom after she had done her own job. Every big house had a stillroom with one stillroom maid or more. The name originated from a room in which a still was kept for the distillation of essences. They made all the cakes, special bread, rolls, scones, preserves and jam, did the morning trays and washed up the coffee cups and dessert plates so they often had to stay up very late at night till these had been brought from the dining-room after dinner was over.

Now Mrs Child lives in Tea Pot Row, Edensor. She made the wedding cakes for my three children. The icing was fairy-like in its beauty, and her skill at this artist's job is unequalled.

The Hierarchy

The formality and the precise divisions of work in a big house led to equally formal modes of address. Housekeepers, cooks and nannies were honorary 'Mrs' whether they were married or not. Ladies' maids were always called 'Miss'—never by their christian names, and properly brought up children would never dream of leaving out the 'Mr' when talking to the butler (of whom they were usually in considerable awe) or any of the menservants unless they were contemporaries, as the footmen might have been. My mother-in-law calls her cook (who has been with her for fifty-three years) and maid by their surnames only, to the intense amusement of my children. In spite of living cheek by jowl under the same roof for nearly half a century the cook and maid never got on to christian-name terms and called each other Miss Woodman and Mrs Weaver till Miss Woodman died in 1976.

The busiest time at Chatsworth was Christmas, when all the daughters and sons-in-law and their children came to stay, as well as my parents-in-law and their children, Billy, Andrew, Elizabeth and Anne. Like everything else in the house the nursery was arranged in order of precedence. The Hartingtons' children came first, had the best rooms and were served first at meals. Next were Captain Evan and Lady Maud Baillie's family of four, Mr Ivan and Lady Blanche Cobbold's four, Mr Harold and Lady Dorothy Macmillan's four, Captain James and Lady Rachel Stuart's three, and Mr Henry and Lady Anne Hunloke's three. Each family brought a nanny and a nursery maid, a lady's maid, a valet and sometimes a chauffeur and a groom as well.

On Christmas Day there were about a hundred and forty people to feed—thirty to forty in the dining-room, twenty in the nursery, up to thirty in the steward's room, up to fifty in the servants' hall, and some meals in the housemaids' room.

The staff parties of the thirties were splendid affairs. They danced in the Great Dining-Room to the band which played in the vestibule, sat out in the Sculpture Gallery and there was a table which ran the length of the Orangery for the buffet. Mrs Tanner ordered meringue cases and brioche rolls from London. These were put on the night train from St Pancras and were fetched from Rowsley at six in the morning to be filled

66

Tenants and employees arriving at the garden party before the wedding of
Lady Rachel Cavendish to the Hon. James Stuart, 1923

and set out for the evening with the more substantial dishes. Two
hairdressers armed with curling tongs came from Baslow and spent all
day coiffing the maids. Dancing went on till four-thirty in the morning,
and no one bothered to go to bed. One of the old guard said to me, 'The
staff party we have now is just a get-together. In the thirties it was a
grand ball.'

Eddie Devonshire, Tenth Duke (1895–1950), my father-in-law

The Tenth Duke

Edward William Spencer (1895–1950)

Eddie Hartington married Lady Mary Cecil (nicknamed Moucher), second daughter of the Fourth Marquess of Salisbury in 1917. After the war was over they had a house in London and stayed at Chatsworth as guests of his parents. They lived at Hardwick for a short time and moved to Churchdale Hall, Ashford-in-the-Water, in 1923. Churchdale was their own house, where Andrew and his brother and sisters spent their childhood.

Eddie was M.P. for West Derbyshire from 1923 till he succeeded his father in 1938 and went to the House of Lords.

My parents-in-law lived at Chatsworth for only a few months. The Duke was Parliamentary Under-Secretary of State for the Dominions from 1936 to 1940, and he and my mother-in-law went on prolonged tours of Australia and South Africa in 1938, the year his father died, and did not move in till Christmas that year.

Mary Duchess (b. 1895) wife of the
Tenth Duke, my mother-in-law

My mother-in-law planned many internal alterations and improve-
ments to the house, and had there been time to carry them out, there is
no doubt she would have made Chatsworth as comfortable and
welcoming as she made Churchdale, Compton Place and 2 Carlton
Gardens. There was a fascinating scheme for a high-speed electric
railway to bring the food from the kitchen to the dining-room, so that it
could arrive hot instead of congealing, but it was never finished.

In August 1939 my parents-in-law gave a series of parties for the
coming of age of their elder son, Billy Hartington. Thousands of people
came over several days of brilliant weather, and by the end of the second
day my mother-in-law's right arm was in a sling from too much hand-
shaking.

A month later war was declared. The contents of the house were
packed away in eleven days—a task almost impossible to imagine, but
carried out with meticulous care by the house carpenters and 'the men',
under the direction of Mr Shimwell. My parents-in-law moved back to
Churchdale, and a girls' public school, Penrhos College, moved in.

The Duke made the arrangement for Penrhos to take the house when
he thought war was inevitable, realising that a girls' school would make
far better tenants than soldiers. Three hundred girls and teachers spent
six years here, sleeping in rows in the passages and the state rooms, and
did their work in the dining-room, drawing-rooms and other downstairs

69

The State Drawing-Room as a dormitory, 1939–1946

sitting-rooms. They must have suffered terribly from the cold, and it must have been nearly impossible for them to keep clean, as there was little hot water, and few places to find it. Yet I often come across Old Girls who spent the war years here, and they seem to have forgotten the draughts and the dirt and politely pretend they enjoyed it.

The breath of many sleeping girls made a lot of fungus grow behind some of the pictures left hanging in their dormitories, and this worried Mr Thompson, but Granny had a theory that the warm human bodies moving the air about the house was wholly beneficial for the building and its contents.

The silk-covered and panelled walls were boarded across, and the best furniture and pictures were piled into the Library. The Memling

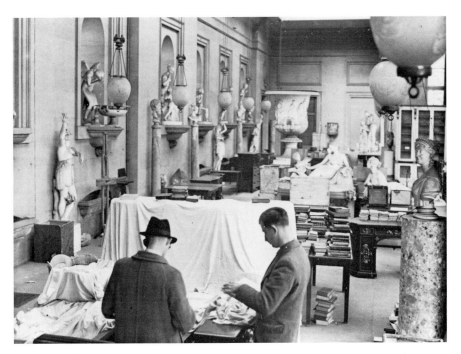

Tom Wragg and wartime muddle in the Orangery

More stored muddle in the Orangery

Penrhos College girls skating on the canal pond in a wartime winter

triptych, the Rembrandts, Van Dycks, Poussins, Reynoldses, Hals and the rest were stacked against the bookshelves and had a lucky escape when a bullet from an American aeroplane on an exercise over the moor above the house found its way through the windows and the shutters and embedded itself in a table, where it remains to this day.

As the war went on my father-in-law spent more time at Compton Place in Eastbourne. He was a Minister in Churchill's government, and so lived in London, and found the weekend train journey to Eastbourne far easier and shorter than coming to Derbyshire on the long and dreary blacked-out Friday evenings. But they came to Churchdale whenever they could.

Eddie Devonshire was not a dressy man. He wore paper collars, and did not possess an overcoat or a macintosh. I can see him now standing in a bitter winter wind on Chesterfield station in a threadbare old London suit, the muffled up porters looking at him with great surprise. Once he was half an hour late for dinner and explained that both his legs had gone through the lining of one leg of some ancient velvet trousers and he could not extricate himself. After Chatsworth was turned into a limited company he opened the Antique Dealer's Fair at Grosvenor House and started his speech by saying he could not think why he had been asked, as the only antiques he owned were the clothes he stood up in.

The first time I saw him was when I went to stay at Churchdale in

William Marquess of Hartington, *b*. 1917, killed in action, 1944, Andrew's brother

Kathleen Kennedy, Marchioness of Hartington (1920–1948)

1938. He wore a grocer's apron over his battered suit and was busy making salmon lures from a collection of feathers given him by women friends off their best hats. He knew the provenance of each one and spent ages choosing what he thought would be irresistible to a fish, muttering, 'Ettie Desborough, Ascot, 1926' or 'Nancy Astor, Buckingham Palace, 1930' while he worked. Then he would try the lures out in his bath, filling it to the brim and putting his head under water while he flicked and jiggled the things on the surface, deciding which he, the guinea-pig salmon, preferred.

Andrew and I were married in London in April 1941. The windows of my father's house in Rutland Gate were blown out by a bomb which fell two nights before the wedding. The glass was swept up, and my mother hung rolls of wallpaper as mocked-up curtains. Red camellias came from Chatsworth, and the reception went on as if nothing had happened.

Andrew was in the Coldstream Guards and while he was stationed in England I followed him around till Emma was born in 1943. His battalion went to Italy in November 1943. Peregrine (nicknamed Stoker or Sto) was born at Churchdale, lent to me by my parents-in-law, in April 1944. Two weeks later Billy Hartington married Kathleen Kennedy, sister of the late President Kennedy. Her father had been the United States Ambassador in London. They had five weeks together before Billy's battalion of the Coldstream Guards was ordered to

France soon after D-Day. On 9 September he was killed in action in Belgium. In 1948 she died in an air crash. They had no children, so the tragic event of Billy's death changed the course of our lives, and Andrew became heir to his father.

After the school left in 1946 the house was empty except for two housemaids, Emily and Annie, who perched in a distant room at the north end.

Careful tenants as Penrhos College and the girls were, the sheer number of them made the house pretty shabby and worn when they left, and very little painting or decorating had been done for twenty-five or thirty years, since the 1914–18 war. After the crushing blow of Billy's death Eddie and Moucher lost heart and did not feel inclined to do much to the house at that time, and even if they had wanted to there was a strict limit of £150 worth of painting allowed by law, and even for that you had to get a permit. They remained at Churchdale, Compton Place and in London.

We lived at the Rookery at Ashford-in-the-Water till 1947, when we moved to Edensor, less than a mile from Chatsworth. Of course we often went across the park to the house and got to know it and the garden intimately. Even at that time, when it was cold, empty and dirty, there was something fascinating and compelling in the atmosphere, and it was always a pleasure and an excitement to explore the shuttered rooms. Although only the two housemaids slept in the house during those years, the carpenters, joiners and plumbers were at work. Once a week the clocks were wound and chimed in unison, sounding through the empty galleries and halls bang on the hour.

In 1948 Andrew's mother and father started to think about re-opening the house to the public (though they never considered going back to live there themselves) and set about finding a housekeeper to organise it and supervise the re-arrangement of the furniture and pictures more or less as they had been in 1939.

They were lucky in their choice. When Kathleen Hartington died in May 1948 she was living in Smith Square and had lately engaged two redoubtable sisters, Hungarian by birth, Ilona and Elisabeth Solymossy, to be cook and housemaid. After Kathleen's death they stayed on in her house as caretakers while its future was decided, and my mother-in-law got to know them well. She offered them the job here and asked them to gather up a team of their acquaintances who were sturdy enough to face

Andrew, myself,
Emma and Sto at
Edensor House, 1948

Staff, Christmas 1964: Ilona Solymossy (seated) and her sister Elisabeth;
the men (left to right): William Bryson, butler; Denis Fisher, comptroller;
Sidney Child, assistant comptroller and husband of Dorothy; Ernest
Grosvenor, outside caterer; Eric Oliver, head house carpenter; John Oliver,
joiner; Jesse Grafton, one of 'the men'; Fred Stone, electrician

the enormous task of cleaning and making ready the house for the opening.

They arrived on 23 August 1948, together with nine of their compatriots, and immediately made their presence felt by setting about the rooms methodically and thoroughly, dressed like Tabitha Twitchit in cotton kerchiefs against the dust, while delicious smells of goulash in the kitchen passage reminded one that the Hungarian takeover was on. They worked through the winter of 1948–9, and the house was ready for the opening at Easter. In spite of petrol rationing 75,000 people came to see it at half a crown each and a shilling for the garden.

Then, in November 1950, the blow fell which changed so drastically the form of the estate. The Duke died suddenly and without warning while at his favourite occupation of chopping wood. He was fifty-five.

Not only did Andrew lose his father, friend and wise counsellor, but he inherited a monstrous problem which took seventeen years to resolve. Death duties of eighty per cent had to be paid on the estate, investments and the works of art which had been collected over the four hundred years since William Cavendish married Bess of Hardwick.

Although he had advice from many people, it was he and he alone who had to decide the best way of raising the millions of pounds which the law demanded. The responsibility for this decision was a heavy one and he was preoccupied by it for years. He pondered and considered the means by which the money could be raised which would have the least bad effect on the collections, the estate and succeeding generations of his family. Chatsworth was always at the centre of his thoughts and his plans. Everything revolved round Chatsworth. His prime object was to save the house and as much of the contents as possible, though it seemed unlikely that either would remain in the ownership, let alone the occupation, of his family. There was much speculation both local and national as to what would become of the place, and all kinds of suggestions were made by all kinds of people.

Sales of land began soon after the Duke's death. The first to go was twelve thousand acres in Dumfriesshire, and this was followed over the next few years by forty-two thousand acres in Derbyshire and town property and woodlands in Sussex. 19 Hill Street (which the Duke bought after 2 Carlton Gardens was hit by a fire bomb) was sold. Compton Place was let to a school after a sale of most of its furniture and books, and its charming kitchen garden grew, instead of vegetables behind espaliered apples and herbaceous borders, some exceedingly ugly blocks of flats.

Nine of the most important works of art in the collection left Chatsworth for ever: Rembrandt's *Philosopher*, Holbein's cartoon of Henry VII and Henry VIII, Rubens' *Holy Family*, Claude's *Liber Veritatis*, the Greek bronze head of Apollo, the Memling Triptych, the tenth-century manuscript Benedictional of St Aethelwold, Van Dyck's Italian sketchbook and the fifteenth-century hunting tapestries. The British Museum took 141 books, over 60 of them printed before 1500. They included fourteen works published by Wynkyn de Worde, Caxton's head printer, of which the British Museum had no copies.

In spite of all this there was still a long, long way to go. Then, in 1953, Andrew had a brilliant idea which solved another great problem—he decided to offer Hardwick Hall, its contents and supporting farm land to the government in lieu of duty. The offer was accepted, and the government handed it over to the National Trust. Bess's surviving masterpiece, one of the most beautiful houses in the world, thus severed its connection with the Cavendishes after fifteen generations, but in doing so it helped to ensure the future of Chatsworth. What remained after the depredations of death duties might support one enormous house, but certainly not two.

The negotiations over Hardwick went on for a long time and the transfer was finally completed in 1959. Meanwhile the proceeds from the other sales were passed on to the Treasury, and as the years went by the vast bill was gradually reduced, and the future of Chatsworth looked a little less bleak.

The final payment of duty was made on 17 May 1967 leaving a huge deficit on the Trustees' income account due to the interest on the outstanding debt which had to be met from estate income over those seventeen years. That deficit was not cleared until 1974, twenty-four years after the death of the Duke.

The Nineteen-Fifties

Meanwhile the day-to-day maintenance of the house went on as usual, but with strict economies. Mr Shimwell and 'the men' looked after the roof and all that was under it, the Solymossys and their compatriots cleaned and mended, scrubbed, polished and tidied. Sometimes they brought forth wonders that had lain beneath other wonders in hopeless heaps of *things* in attic room after attic room. They made order out of disorder.

After they had been here a few years one was less likely to open a drawer and discover, as I once did, a miniature of Georgiana, a Women's Institute programme of 1932, a bracelet given by Pauline Borghese to the Bachelor Duke to hide a crack in the marble arm of a statue of Venus, and a crystal wireless set.

The first big change Andrew made to the house was to have all the plate glass windows on the south front replaced by small panes. We thought the plate-glass windows were a great mistake of the Bachelor Duke's, as much of an insult to the building as navy blue asphalt paths would be to the garden, and they made the house look blind and dreary from the outside. There was enough seasoned oak in the building yard to do the job.

Maltby and the joiners, including Eric Oliver, now Comptroller, made all the new window frames—twenty-four of them—and filled them with bevelled glass, so few people guess they were made in the 1950s. Thirty years later these huge windows work perfectly and run up and down at the touch of a finger.

In 1955 Hugo Read, the agent, suggested to Andrew that as the house had to be looked after, aired and cleaned, and someone had to live in it, why not consider going to live there ourselves? I suppose we had talked about it, but I do not think either of us had ever thought that it was a practical possibility. The idea sank in slowly, and we began to think about which rooms we could use and what alterations would be necessary.

It was at this time that I began to realise the extraordinary devotion to the house which had been shown by the comptroller Mr Shimwell and his staff since the family left in 1939.

We were warned that estimates for alterations would be meaningless, as every old house sprouts dry rot when unseen bits are delved into, and therefore we must expect the cost to be double the estimate, or more. But such was the care and attention that had been lavished on the building by Willie Shimwell and Bill Maltby that the roof and every timber were sound, much to the surprise of our advisers.

Gradually the plans were made and the decision to go ahead was taken. Two big builders' huts were put up outside the West Front Door and work started in 1958.

The alterations took eighteen months, and in November 1959 we moved in. It would be wearisome to describe all we did in detail. I find nothing so boring as sagas about other people's central heating, and I have never understood how drains work or why water comes out when you turn on a tap. When Mr Shimwell tried to explain he might as well have been talking in Japanese. All these mysteries seem to me to be as strange and clever as how stairs can carry people by the ton without collapsing or why ceilings stay up. I just hope the house will be warm and that the bath-water will be hot and the lavatories will work.

But I could not help watching the miracle wrought, seeing copper pipes, twisted like giant's intestines, wrapped in and around the new bathrooms, mysterious boxes full of electric magic, a large hole open to the sky for six months in the wall of the closet by the Red Velvet Room to contain the drain for a new bath and lavatory where water had never reached before, and the huge boiler-room at the far end of the house which burns coke (chosen because we are near coal mines and far from oil wells) and works it all.

When we had decided on the rooms we would use and the various routes of getting to and from them, and settled where the new kitchen would be and how to fit in the new bathrooms, someone suggested we should find an interior decorator.

When I was young I watched my mother doing up whatever house we were living in and making it far prettier on far less money than those of friends who employed professionals to do the job, and I felt that I could probably do as she did, and so, for two reasons, we decided against employing a decorator. The first was that I cannot imagine living among someone else's taste, and the second that I cannot see the point of paying someone to do something I can do myself.

I had wonderful help. Andrew gave me a completely free hand and never criticised even if he did not always agree with my ideas. John Page was our architect. He did what I realise is very boring for an architect, making bathrooms and kitchens and all the things which do not show and are extremely tricky and tiresome to fit in to an old building, like hiding radiators, which means panelling brought forward a few inches and such tricks of the trade, which make the observer think nothing has been changed. All this he did with patience and taste, and I shall always be grateful to him.

The painting was done by the Chesterfield firm of Alan Brayshaw, Ltd. The foreman, Eddie Greenwood, and I worked closely together on room after room, planning the programme and the colours. For years there were sample boards leaning against walls with the variations of colours clearly set out so we made no mistakes.

Eddie was a joy to work with, a perfectionist, whose wish was to interpret the ideas of his client, which he did without fail. He was always smiling, even after he swallowed a mouthful of tintacks which he had rashly parked between his lips while using both hands to hang some lining paper. We all waited anxiously for news of the tintacks and were greatly relieved when a message came the next morning to say there was no longer any need to worry.

Mr Shimwell took infinite trouble to get what I asked for when it was needed and on time, something which was difficult then and would be almost impossible now.

Miss Feeney, sempstress daughter of the venerable dairy maid at Lismore, made curtains and covers by the dozen, always to her meticulously high standard. She copied the worn-out hangings of four-poster beds with intricate sunbursts of pleats and rosettes and swags, darned old silk and covered the most precious fragments of brittle and broken brocade with tulle, slightly coloured by dipping in tea, which holds the old stuff in place when it is too dead to mend.

The Solymossy sisters matched up pairs of this and that, brought out curtains and carpets stored for twenty years, and attacked our rooms as they had attacked the public part of the house ten years before. We put back the furniture as it had been before the war wherever it seemed right, and Mr Maltby knew exactly where each piece belonged. The task was complicated by the addition of a lot of furniture from 2 Carlton Gardens, some from Compton Place and a few pieces from Hardwick, as

Chairs in an attic, 1982

well as that which had come from Chiswick when it was sold to
Brentford Council in 1929.

For this reason Chatsworth has got more furniture and pictures in it
than at any time in its history. In the attics there are two, and sometimes
three, layers of chairs piled on temporary wooden shelves. You become
practised at remembering which set of chairs is where, but there is still a
huge game of pelmanism to be played, as one or two strayed members of
a set are often spotted as far apart as the wardens' tea room at
Chatsworth, at Bolton Abbey, or in our London house.

Repainting nearly all the rooms and re-arranging the furniture was a
fascinating task and made me familiar with the house from attics to
cellars as nothing else could have done. It forced me to look at the rooms
and their contents as if for the first time and to pay proper attention to
detail, because if I did not decide what was to be done no one else was going
to.

I am thankful that I was thirty-eight when I found myself making
these decisions. The house had had time to impress its powerful
character on me and prevented the wholesale use of pink paint, which
was my only idea of decoration when I first grew up.

Painting and rearranging rooms will never end, but the major task of
our part of the house was finished in the autumn of 1959 (though
rewiring went on for three more winters) and with a certain feeling of
achievement we packed up Edensor House after twelve years there and
crossed the river to our new abode.

Living in Chatsworth

We moved in the autumn of 1959. The intense pleasure of living in the house and of actually using the rooms we had visited so often for the purpose for which they were built, waking up to the wide view across the park and being surrounded by so much beauty is our good fortune, and something of which I am acutely aware, and will never take for granted however many years I may live here.

The joys and the problems of living in a huge house are all magnified. Everything is bigger than life-size, the indoor distances, the faraway meals, the long passages and stairs for luggage all add to the complications of life. A bag put down in a rare bit of house can be lost for months. The master key can be forgotten in an attic door till panic sets in. It is a terrible place to house train a puppy. Letting a dog out in the night is quite a performance, including the complicated unlocking of monster doors. On this inescapable errand of a dog-owner I sometimes meet the night-watchman with his steady tread in the silent dark and the beam of his torch like the Dong with a Luminous Nose, *a single lurid light*. We reassure each other. 'I'm just putting the dog out.' 'Oh, I wondered who it was.' And we go our different ways.

On the good side children can roller-skate for miles without going out of doors; on a wet day you can walk for hours, be entertained and keep dry, gramophone, piano and loud singers can blast away in the drawing-room without fear of waking angry sleepers. And there is always escape from people.

You lose things, but you never know what you may find. Once, on a winter afternoon when it was getting dark, I journeyed to the last room of the East Attics to look for something. It is quite a trek to get there—down the Book Passage to the Bachelor Passage, up the stone stairs, past the lamp cupboards, turn right and it is the third room on the right. I opened the door and stopped dead, amazed to see an old man sitting among piles of books reading under a strong lamp. I was so surprised I said something like, 'I'm so sorry to disturb you' and fled back the way I had come. I have no idea who he was or what he was doing, and for all I know he may still be there.

In all its history Chatsworth has never been lived in for so many months on end as it is now. And it is open for people to see round on more days in the year than ever before. This is both good and bad for the place; good in as much as it keeps it alive, and bad in that constant use inevitably wears away the very things people come to see.

I used to think you could arrange one of the big rooms upstairs, and that it could be frozen like a photograph, and that nothing need be changed as long as it was kept clean. I was wrong. Curtains, bed hangings, coverings on furniture, silk on walls, fade and perish with alarming speed, furniture, leather bindings (like the beasts from which they are made) must be fed, paintings on walls and ceilings restored, carpets mended if old and beautiful, replaced if new and much walked on. To keep rooms in good order when they are open for people to see is a constant work which does not show except that it halts deterioration. It is like running to stand still.

In the house and out of doors vigilance and maintenance, unseen and unsung, are the order of the day's work. Nothing is permanent. Lead on the roof wears thin, and a hole the size of a pinhead lets in rain which can soon turn into dry rot. Stone, especially when bedded the wrong way of its grain, flakes, and the weather finds the weak places and scoops them out as if with a giant spoon. Garden paths pounded by half a million feet a year (a quarter of a million people with about two feet each) are flattened to rock bottom and their drains must be cleaned out or grand canyons appear after every storm. Woodworm, death-watch beetle, fire, water, snow, frost, wind and sun (All Ye Works of the Lord, in fact) each does its special harm. Every householder is aware of these nuisances, but they are magnified at Chatsworth because of its size.

The roof is 1.3 acres. There are 175 rooms, of which 51 are very big indeed, 96 of more or less normal size, 21 kitchens and workshops and 7 offices connected by 3,426 feet of passages, 17 staircases and 359 doors — all lit by 2,084 electric light bulbs.

There are 397 external window-frames, 62 internal window-frames, 5 roof lanterns and 60 roof lights with a grand total of 7,873 panes of glass. 24 baths, 52 wash-hand basins, 29 sinks, 53 lavatories and 6 wash-ups complete the unusual statistics.

The total cubic living space in Chatsworth is 1,704,233 cubic feet. The total cubic living space in a first-time buyer's modern two-bedroomed house is 4,726 cubic feet. So you could fit 365 such houses into

Chatsworth. The Painted Hall could contain 10.45, the Great Dining-Room 8.3, and the Sculpture Gallery 14.23 houses.

I have lived here long enough to have seen inevitable changes, but probably fewer than in most places. I have heard the 'experts' juggle the attributions of works of art with monotonous regularity, and watched fashion change in what is admired and what is denigrated, and seen the most ordinary household things of a few years ago become museum pieces. Last year I heard a boy of about nine shout to his friend as he passed a writing-table, 'Look! A pen nib!'

Ever since Mr Strong was appointed librarian in 1893 there has been a steady stream of scholars to find 'source material', and works of art and curiosities have always been, and I hope always will be, lent to exhibitions all over the world. The biggest single show mounted from here was called 'Treasures of Chatsworth' and went to five art galleries in America between September 1979 and July 1980, and on its return to this country was shown at the Royal Academy in the winter of 1980–1.

Andrew has more than compensated for the hundred years of little bought. His purchases have made a tremendous impact on the collection, and he has added some remarkably beautiful objects, notably the Lucian Freud portraits, the Samuel Palmer watercolours, Angela Conner's sculptures, illustrated books, and many other things besides, from paintings and miniatures to minerals. His room is littered with unhung pictures and unopened parcels from bookshops. His time here will not be forgotten by his successors.

There are two librarians now, and never a day goes by but they get a heap of letters asking all kinds of questions often on the most obscure subjects.

Chatsworth has a tradition of long service. In 1963 Andrew gave a party for people who had worked on the Derbyshire estate for twenty-five years or longer. 175 people came, of whom 123 had done twenty-five years or more and 52 had completed over forty years. Since then awards have been given at the staff party every year and by 1981 166 people have received tankards (twenty-five years) and 91 have a pair of silver candlesticks (forty years).

There must be something salubrious about the air in these parts, as the Baslow medical practice knew only three doctors in the 116 years between 1862 when Dr Wrench arrived, till 1978 when Dr Sinclair Evans retired.

1963: party for people who had served the house for over 25 years.
Some of the guests, including (front row, left to right) Nurse Parry, village
nurse; Miss Woodman; Miss Webb; Mr Thompson and (far right) Mr Maltby.
Andrew, Sto, myself and my mother-in-law at the foot of the steps

Chatsworth and the Visitor

The house has been open for people to see round since it was built. There are no detailed records of the early years, but accounts of travellers from the time of Celia Fiennes (1622–1741) and Defoe (1660–1731) onwards make it clear that all interested people could see the main rooms and the garden.

In the eighteenth century the family lived mostly in London, but the housekeeper had instructions to show people round, and when the Fifth Duke and Georgiana were here there were 'open days' when dinner was provided for anyone passing by. An inn (now the Estate Office and Club) was built in 1775 for the convenience of the sightseers.

When the Sixth Duke was making his alterations and additions to the house it attracted much attention, and more and more people came to see what was happening. The Great Conservatory was finished and planted in 1840. Nothing like this airy palace of glass and iron had ever been seen before, and the newest wonder of the Peak created a sensation.

The following extract from *The Mirror of Literature and Amusement* of February 1844 shows that all were welcome at Chatsworth:

The Duke of Devonshire allows all persons whatsoever to see the mansion and grounds every day in the year, Sundays not excepted, from 10 in the morning till 5 in the afternoon. The humblest individual is not only shown the whole, but the Duke has expressly ordered the waterworks to be played for everyone without exception. This is acting in the true spirit of great wealth and enlightened liberality; let us add, also, in the spirit of wisdom.

In 1849 the opening of the Midland Railway from Derby to Rowsley, three miles away down the Derwent valley, made Chatsworth accessible to the population of the great manufacturing towns, and by this time 80,000 people were visiting the house during the summer. This number was exceeded when the railway reached Manchester (1863). No charge was made, and all the rooms were shown except the Duke's private apartments on the West Front.

This printed account from a scrapbook in the library describes an 'Excursion to Chatsworth by Rail from Derby, June 1849':

A party of 500 respectable, orderly, and well-dressed individuals have this day

The Queen and the Prince Consort arriving at Chatsworth, 1843

(Wednesday) been conducted with the greatest possible attention and politeness, by order of His Grace the Duke of Devonshire, through the stately and magnificent apartments of Chatsworth, its conservatories, grottos, pleasure grounds, and gardens, to their unspeakable gratification, instruction and delight. Such an instance of condescension is perhaps without a parallel, and that which gave additional effect to the whole was, that all this took place while His Grace was at Chatsworth, and who, we understand, with that expansive benevolence and kindheartedness which the humblest person could appreciate, gave orders that everything should be done, without even the expectation of fee or reward from his servants, that could reasonably contribute to the day's enjoyment on the part of the visitors.

The spacious park and cricket ground were at their disposal for *pic nic* parties and amusements; whilst the playing fountains and flowing cascades in all directions gave indisputable proof that none felt more happy or more anxious than the noble Duke himself did in dispensing so much happiness to others.

But we should have observed that this excursion party was from Derby, and is the first pleasure trip that has passed along the Amber Gate and Rowsley Railway. It consisted of nearly 30 first and second class carriages, and the journey was performed in one hour, the day throughout proving extremely fine and agreeable.

At Rowsley, on arrival of the train between 8 and 9 a.m., a most animated scene presented itself, for although the spirited arrangements of Mr. Greaves

87

and Mr. Jepson had furnished a good supply of omnibuses, coaches, and carriages, to convey persons at sixpence each to Chatsworth, they were scarcely prepared for so strong a muster, and consequently some had to walk or remain till the vehicles returned. This obstacle was ultimately got over without much inconvenience, and a long line of carriages proceeded on their way to Chatsworth; Mr. Paxton having previously arrived at the station and given orders that they might take the shorter route, or private drive through the park. Having now arrived with light hearts and happy faces at the beautiful entrance gates, very little delay was experienced.

By an admirable arrangement which secured comfort and convenience to all parties, the visitors were admitted in companies of 20 each at intervals of two or three minutes, so that one party might be in advance of, and not interfere with another. Each group was then conducted by one of the domestics through the entrance hall, chapel, drawing room, State apartments, staircases, sculpture gallery, the orangery, etc. etc., when another of His Grace's servants joined the party and led them to the grottos, the grand conservatory, Italian gardens and pleasure grounds. It is due to the servants of this noble establishment here to remark that the greatest civility, readiness, and anxiety was manifested by them throughout the day in explaining and rendering intelligible to many a wondering mind and curious observer, the various objects of attraction; —and although it was understood the admission would be strictly free, many persons offered gratuities, but we believe in every instance they were respectfully declined. During the admission of the visitors to Chatsworth His Grace was observed by some of the parties promenading on the grounds, and about two o'clock he took an airing in his carriage. This, to many, was the crowning gratification, for to see the noble Duke as well as Chatsworth, on one and the same day, was to consummate their happiness, and render that a day never to be forgotten. We heard several remark as the carriage rolled by, they never felt such a mental struggle between duty and inclination, as they did at that moment; —their inclination was to cheer the Duke as he passed, but fearing it might violate the rules of strict propriety, they restrained their feelings; we feel pretty certain, however, if the scattered groups pic-nicing in all directions of the park at the time, had been aware of it, they would have assembled together and His Grace would have received from men, women, and children, a round of the heartiest cheers that could possibly be given by a grateful and admiring people, despite all the rules of etiquette, and this simply because the people 'could not help it'.

The Seventh Duke (d 1891) kept the house open to visitors, and so did his successor. 11,351 people came during Whit week 1884, and this figure remained more or less constant for the next twenty years and is not very different from present day numbers for that week. A record day was Whit Monday 1905 when 4,550 people came here.

After the Ninth Duke succeeded in 1908 a small charge was made, which, after paying the guides (who were estate pensioners), was given to local hospitals. In the 1930s the charge was a shilling for adults and sixpence for children and about a thousand pounds was raised for the hospitals annually.

I believe the tour of the house is the longest of any house which is open. It involves stamina of mind and body. Besides the length on the flat, getting on for half a mile, if the Scots Rooms and the Theatre are included, there are 101 steps up and 60 down,* so by the time the visitor has reached the Orangery he is punch-drunk and ready to believe anything. If you tell your victim the two-foot-high quartz crystal found in the rock when the Simplon Pass was made is the biggest diamond in the world he is apt to nod obediently in agreement.

People can go round in their own time because there are no guides. Fourteen-year-old schoolboys fly through (shades of Art Buchwald and 'How to do the Louvre in seven minutes') and aged professors on two sticks can take as many hours as they like. I feel sorry for the tourists who are funnelled through Chatsworth and Haddon on the same day, with Hardwick in reserve just in case there is time. Sometimes our own guests are tortured in this way.

In 1976 we had the great pleasure of a visit from Mrs Lady Bird Johnson, widow of the American President, and her daughter, Linda. A clever woman of immense sympathy and charm, she looked round this house, gardens and farms, the Peak District (where she was greatly intrigued by the network of stone walls which enclose the small fields), Haddon and Hardwick in two short days. Even *her* energy was waning, but as she left to drive to London, I said, 'Do go and look at Sudbury Hall on your way south. It is so lovely, and well worth seeing.' Upon which Linda said, 'Oh don't suggest it. *Mother's just about housed out.*' I'm afraid a lot of people get housed out after seeing the local sights, and friends who have come for a restful weekend in the country go back to London very tired.

*You emerge on a higher level.

The South Front with the Emperor Fountain

PART TWO

A Tour of the House

Broadstairs, Kent.

Tenth October 1851.

My Dear Duke of Devonshire,

As I travelled from Chesterfield in the Railway carriage, I read the little book I now return, with a pleasure I can scarcely express to you. It was so like going over the house again with you, and hearing you talk about it, that it had a perfect charm for me. And besides this, I found it in itself so natural and unaffected, so gracefully sensible, and altogether so winning and so good, that I read it through from the first page to the last, without once laying it aside.

I could mention some things in it which it would require a very nice art to do as well in fiction. The little suggestive indications of some of the old servants, and old rooms—and the childish associations—are perfect little pieces of truth. I know that lingering old smell of the spirit lamp, for instance, so well!

The American Hobbs could do nothing so agreeable or a thousandth part so agreeable with any lock in the world, as you have done with that lock wherein the man's hat must be pulled over his eyes. It is quite a spring-description. Touched in the right place and done with.

I meant to have told you how much I was moved by the tribute to Paxton—rendered with such a noble earnestness. But I am afraid you would begin to think me a victim to the habit of authorship, and remorselessly inflicting on you a regular Review of the book.

I must, however, thank you from my heart for all your kindness and hospitality, and assure you that among your 'Troops of friends', there cannot be one more obliged to you and attached to you than I am. I feel as if there were a sort of boastfulness in writing so much, even for your eyes, but I cannot help it.

My Dear Duke of Devonshire

Ever Faithfully Yours

Charles Dickens

A letter from Charles Dickens to the Sixth Duke, 10 October 1851

A Tour of the House

The Bachelor's Handbook

For a long time I have wanted to publish the Sixth (Bachelor) Duke's *Handbook of Chatsworth* which he wrote in 1844 in the form of a letter to his sister Harriet Cavendish, who married Lord Granville. The only book about the house written since then is Francis Thompson's *History of Chatsworth*, published in 1949, which is an invaluable work of scholarship, but concentrates on the building rather than the people and things in it. As about eight million people have come to see the place since it was reopened in 1949, it is perhaps time to have a closer look. First the Bachelor Duke will tell us something of what it all looked like in 1844 and then I shall fill in rather more of what happened in the next hundred and fifty years, several wars and five dukes later, to bring it up to date.*

The *Handbook* takes you round the house through rooms both public and private. The pictures, furniture, tapestries, china, sculptures and books have been moved countless times since 1844. They still wander about the house and to and from exhibitions in a most disconcerting way. Some have come from other houses, some have gone for ever to pay death duties, but the extraordinary thing is how much of what is described in the *Handbook* is in the house and instantly recognisable now, even such perishables as curtains and carpets. It gives a feeling of permanence to read of this and that and look up from the book and see the objects in front of you, or to study the Hunt watercolours of interiors of 1828 and be able to find nearly everything portrayed in them.

As happened with most of the English familes who have great collections, there was a long pause after the 1850s when nothing except the more or less obligatory portraits of the reigning dukes and their wives was bought. Where are the Pre-Raphaelites, the Impressionists, the Post-Impressionists, the Surrealists and the Abstracts? Why are there no Lalique vases, no Art Deco jewellery or Charles Rennie Mackintosh

*The extracts quoted here (in italics) amount to slightly less than half of what the Bachelor Duke wrote about Chatsworth in his *Handbook*.

Lady Granville (1785–1862)   The Bachelor Duke aged 15

furniture? Were they not admired? Would they have been considered
unwarranted extravagances? Or did the Seventh, Eighth, Ninth and
Tenth Dukes and Louise, Evie and Moucher just think there was enough
of everything? Too late to discover now, but I should dearly love to know
the reason for the complete drawing in of horns by people who, till then,
were game to buy anything that took their eye.

In 1844 the Bachelor Duke had no such inhibitions, and we will set off
on the tour of the house and garden a few paces behind him and his sister
Lady Granville.

Chatsworth, July 18th, 1844.

Dearest Harriet,

*I am gratified by your wish of knowing something about Chatsworth—as
it is in my occupation, and as it was in my recollections; and if our
grandfathers would but have written so, as they would have done if they had
had inquisitive sisters, how amusing and useful it would have been to me!*

*My plan is to suppose that you are just arrived, and that I show you every
room and corner of the house; leaving Granville corner, which is on the
outside, to be described when we have done within doors.*

*It rains, and you are surprised not to be wet on getting out of the carriage.
That is owing to the new porch, built in wood, looking like stone; and to be
built in stone some day or other, having been hastily put up for the Queen's
visit, in December, 1843.*

When it rained and Lady Granville got out of her carriage under a new
porch she was lucky. She would get wet now, as the porch was never built

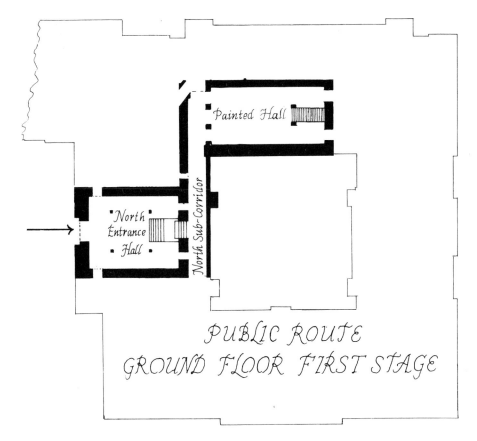

Painted Hall

North
Entrance
· Hall ·

North Sub-Corridor

PUBLIC ROUTE
GROUND FLOOR FIRST STAGE

in stone as promised, but quietly disintegrated and was pulled down by the Ninth Duke in 1911.

All her fellow visitors who come to see the house arrive by this entrance, and sometimes they get very wet indeed as they walk from the Lodge after leaving their cars.

The North Entrance Hall°*

This was the kitchen in former days—in my grandfather's time; and the entrance to the house was in the corner, where the billiard-room is now. We can remember this hall, with two fireplaces where they now are leading to the rigours of the inner courtyard, in the open air; with an open colonnade, and

*The symbol ○ indicates that a room is open to the public, ● that it is closed, and ◗ that it is occasionally open.

95

The North Entrance Hall, watercolour by William Hunt, 1827

a precipitous descent in the corner, guarded by a few iron bars, by which the two single habitable morning rooms were gained. A charming fountain was in the centre of the paved court, with Arion, on a dolphin, pouring water into its leaden lining—leaking, imperfect: but what joy it was to fish with an iron prong for the subaqueous bolt which made the dolphin spout more vehemently! All this is gone: the marble exterior, being worn out, was condemned, and it is now a large flower-basket before the old greenhouse; while Arion is perched upon the top of one of the removed columns of the corridor, before which he used to figure.

The two ancient statues, Domitian and Agrippina, are from the hall at Wanstead.* The gilt lead vases, that hinder people from tumbling through the openings from the corridor, were in the Painted Hall here. The bust of Jupiter, on the chimney-piece, had its place in the awful room up-stairs, that formerly was called the Den. It frowned from the top of a lofty bookcase.

Four busts on the black columns appear to be ancient. I am very fond of one of them, which had the united purpose of a likeness and a monument combined, by a freedman, (Libertus) for his Liberta, whose graceful name

*At the sale of the contents of Wanstead House, Essex, in 1822 the Bachelor Duke bought many lots.

The State Dressing-Room with the view from its windows

Baby-carriages and sledge on the Great Staircase landing

The statue of Mercury on the Great Staircase

was Sozusa. The black marble has lost its colour, which shows its inferiority to the marble of the more recently worked quarries at Ashford Rookery. On the steps are two colossal busts; one magnificent of Alexander, found at Burlington House; the other, an acquisition of mine at Smyrna, to which Campbell, the sculptor, has supplied a nose.

The room is greatly improved since the days of cookery: the shafts of the stone columns were in existence then; but the capitals, architrave, frieze and cornice, and the steps are new. Through the left-hand window you can just see the arch that used to be the single entrance to Old Chatsworth. On your right stood three regular buildings, not unseemly offices, projecting more into the approach than the present servants' hall—bad within, and not fit to be retained. On the left hand was an impervious wood. On entering it, one found meat-safes, and larders and carpenters'-pits, and dog-kennels, and dark recesses for lumber: then a wall, concealed towards the west by shrubs; and, on the other side of it, a gravel walk, which, leaving the three yew-trees, went up on arches to a mount, and over the solitary gateway to the pleasure-ground. What arrivals and departures this room recalls to me! what different ranks and persons—from the great of the earth, coming and going, to the charity children, engaged at their plum-pudding, inspected by our grandmother, Lady Spencer, from above; while a poor man brought a tame hare, to show to the Marchesino—so tame, that it bit the end of his finger nearly off, the scar of which is evident to this day.

Now, dear lady, as our best correspondent calls you, you know your fate, Leave off, if the details and the twaddle tire you; for, if the lobby says so much, what will not the rooms do?

The hall is almost unchanged since the Handbook was written. The statues are there, and the gilt lead vases still guard the openings from the corridor above.

The footmen's chairs are by the fireplace. Landseer's *Bolton Abbey in the Olden Time*, with its unlikely bag from a very strange day's shooting, is on one wall.* The splendid frame of a Rubens taken for death duties in the 1950's now encloses *Diana with her Nymphs* by Maratta and Dughet. Here, in a wicked draught, sits the unfortunate seller of guide-books.

*The Bachelor Duke writes: 'Landseer's Bolton Abbey might be any other abbey: its immense success as a painting reconciled me to his not having made what I gave him a commission for—namedly, a representation of the place. He went there, and saw, and admired; and everybody was satisfied, except poor old Rev. Carr, who thought it a take-in. Landseer got Sir Augustus Calcot to sit for the Abbot's head.'

Bolton Abbey in the Olden Time by Sir Edwin Landseer, 1834

The North Sub-Corridor°

On coming into this passage, you are struck with exceeding beauty of the pavement. It is composed chiefly of ancient marbles, and was the work of Leonardi, a poor man, who lives at the Forum at Rome. When it was first laid down in the brightness of its polish, it was difficult to make anybody tread upon it.

You ask what can have made me put so gorgeous a floor in this plain stone gallery. I shall tell you. It is to divert the attention and eyes of the arrivers from a grand defect in the entrance: on reaching the top of the steps, if they had nothing else to think of, they would not only perceive that the door to the court is not in the centre, but that the irregularities extend to both fronts in the inner court. Sir Jeffry Wyatville had endless difficulties to meet and overcome, and began, encouraged by me, with the error of keeping the old proportions of the basement and first floor.

The three central windows of the basement on your left were niches containing smoky stone statues, now moved to distant parts of the pleasure-ground. I find in an old account-book that £280 was charged for the trophies on the wall. Of the fountain and Arion I have already spoken. The golden balcony came from the steps that were taken down in the south front.

To return to the interior of the corridor. The brackets are made of cast iron, copied from those in the large room at Devonshire House. Four of the busts came from there, and appear to be ancient. The fragments of hands and the bust of Faustina belonged to Canova, and were bought by me, with many others, soon after his death, of his brother, the Abbate. The fat seated woman is bad, but she fell in my way at Athens, where so little can be got that I became less fastidious. The little bust of a laughing Faun was a great favourite of my Mother's, and was always on the chimney-piece of her dressing-room in London. The carpet portières are, I think, very successful, and embellish and warm this once dreary passage.

Alas, the visitor is no longer struck by the 'exceeding beauty of the pavement', as it is covered by a boring red carpet which haunts him throughout the tour of the house till he reaches the Sculpture Gallery. I would dearly like to take the carpet away from here, but I am assured the pavement could not stand the continuous pounding of feet. But probably the eyes of the beholders would not be sharp enough to take in the reason for its existence. How many people, coming here for the first time, notice that the door into the courtyard is not in the middle, and neither are those opposite?

We have put back the fountain in the courtyard. When the stone basin was filled with earth and bedded-out plants it was dreary in the extreme, as no sun reached it. The watery plan is more lively, but through unwonted lack of confidence I caused the vase to be placed too low in the basin, and one day this must be put right.

The Painted Hall°

The former steps here were decidedly much handsomer than the present ones. They were a double flight, not projecting nearly so far, and showing the alabaster doorway in the middle that still remains, though concealed, in its old place; but they were exceedingly steep and inconvenient, and the gallery round the room (an afterthought) could not have been added to them. It used to be a dark, dismal place, though the painted walls and ceiling were then as now; but there was no windows in the basement: a deal wainscot, painted yellow, surrounded it. Upstairs, the communication has been of such real advantage, that we must not lament the loss of Cæsar's frightened attendants, who made way for the openings to the landing-place of the oak staircase.

The marble floor has been altered and relaid. It was ugly in its former state, with a large lozenge in the middle; and the only ornament was in the four angles, which now form the interval between the Roman pavement in the North Corridor, and the black and white one.

Having completed the reconstruction, the Bachelor Duke signed it over the chimneypiece:

> Aedes has paternas dilectissimas anno
> libertatis anglicae MDCLXXXVIII institutas
> Gul. S. Devoniae Dux anno MDCCCXI haeres
> accepit anno moeroris sui MDCCCXL perfecit.

(William Spencer, Duke of Devonshire, inherited this most beautiful house from his father in the year 1811, which had been begun in the year of the English liberty 1688, and completed in the year of his bereavement 1840.)

His beloved niece Blanche had just died, hence the bereavement.

The sad inscription painted on the marble slab, and intended to be inlaid with the red marble of Derbyshire, was written, at my desire, by the Rev Francis Hodgson, now Provost of Eton, and was submitted by us to Mr. Luttrell for approbation, that we might feel secure as to the Latinity. Still, an incorrect copy got into the newspapers, ill recollected, probably, by some wandering pedant; and it brought upon me the infliction of letters from anonymous and conceited commentators.

The table came from Wanstead—that is, its legs did; and its top is in the state dining-room, a large slab from Ashford replacing it here, so that it has doubled itself in my possession.

In the Caicque I have reposed on the Bosphorus, and never shall it have the indignity of floating on inferior waters. During quarantine at Malta, it was thought necessary to remove the leather thongs by which the ponderous oars were secured to its sides.

The Painted Hall, 1982

The First Duke's staircase in the Painted Hall, watercolour by William Hunt, 1827

The Bachelor Duke's staircase and galleries in the Painted Hall before the 1912 alterations, showing the hall table from Wanstead

This hall remained unchanged till 1912, when Granny Evie and the architect W. H. Romaine-Walker replaced the Bachelor Duke's steep staircase by the present grandiose affair. They scrapped the wooden galleries and made a new one of stone, on the west side only. The Bromsgrove Guild copied Tijou's ironwork here. Right as she was to do away with his straight and ugly stairs, it seems strange to me that she did not put back the First Duke's much prettier curved double flight, as not only would they have looked better but they would have allowed more space than the ponderous stony mass which protrudes so far over the floor. Every time I go into the Painted Hall I regret these stairs, and at the Christmas Party, at a concert, or any function held here, I rue the space they occupy.

Twice a year we have 'coffee mornings' in the Painted Hall for local charities, sure money-raisers and all over in two hours. I think the reason for their success is that our rooms on the first floor are open. People who may have been round the State Rooms many times are naturally more interested to see rooms which are used every day, and they always remark on how 'homely' and 'lived in' they are, which is a polite way of saying they are very untidy.

We can now go up the stairs to these first floor rooms of ours, leaving the rest of the visitors to carry on up to the second floor.

The Great Staircase○

It was necessary to insert iron beams here to give security; the scrolls, like brackets, are also made of iron. The upper flight remains untouched, so you can compare the two, and I hope the old appearance has not suffered much. A little varnish brought to light the chiaro oscuro paintings on the wall. I was sorry to lose the tipsy satyr's head; that was condemned as an addition, but had its merit, or its fun.

Another supporting beam has been put in, steel this time. There is some unfinished decoration on the high stone walls of these stairs, signs of changes of mind of the First Duke. He finished up with sculptures by Cibber and grisaille paintings pretending to be sculpture. These have become horribly dark and dirty, and I'm sure were not meant to look like they do today. I tried tapestry over them, and it didn't look bad, but I gave it up and left the walls as they are.

The baby carriages and the little sleigh fascinate every generation of children. The one with a collar and traces made of snakes was designed by William Kent for the Third Duke's children and was pulled by a goat. The chintz-lined pram was made for Georgiana's elder daughter.

The North (Book) Corridor●

Over the doors at the ends are the panel landscapes, that were in the present library.

Remark a curious view of old Chatsworth, the stand unsheltered and bare, the whole difficult to realize; but a piece of needlework brought from Hardwick, where it had long served for a screen, has been framed and placed opposite, as an appropriate illustration of the picture. It is surrounded by a border of the Cavendish snakes, and it is probably the work of Lady Shrewsbury, possibly of the Queen of Scots.

More and yet more books. One has a damaged spine, caused by a piece of metal which sped through the air and through the window when Paxton's Great Conservatory was blown up in 1919.

The Red Room, North●

Of all the friends, and fashionables, and family lodged here, I shall only record Marie Caroline, Duchesse de Berri, who, passing through Derbyshire in 1830, was invited by me, and came attended by Madame de Bouillé and the Count Mesnard. You remember well her visit; and that, though she had before, in her splendour, made herself as little interesting as possible, the reverses and her quiet courage made us feel for her in the contrast she then underwent. She looked, to my mind, much better in a plain white gown, having asked for two or three dahlias by way of ornament for her hair, than when rigged out by Paris celebrities. She drove about the country, and went to see Haddon, and we little foresaw such adventures as her disguises and chimney concealments in the following year. She was in good spirits, and wanted to dance, but Mesnard forbade that.

During one winter, owing to repairs below, this became the dining-room, we mounting afterwards to the Green Room upstairs. The cumbrous state bed was made for Devonshire House, but soon was transferred to Chatsworth.

The lower Bow is bed-room no longer: it has the advantage of a bath close at hand. If its neighbour had had dinners, you can certify that it had its breakfasts to boast of.

We made this the Day Nursery and sacrificed the red flock paper which was dark and very dirty. The Regency cupboard was a fixture from Devonshire House, highly unsuitable for a nursery as King George IV, a great friend of Georgiana and constant visitor at Devonshire House, used

Statue of Jean-Jacques Rousseau, described by the Bachelor Duke as 'the great alarmer of infant kind'. It still is.

to go through its doors to visit Mrs Fitzherbert in the next room there.

The Lower Plough* and Den•

The lower Plough has become a private morning room for me. It contains a very curious old dark mirror, and charming prints from Paul Delaroche and Leopold Robert. It opens now, but did not formerly, into the Den: the access to that was from the passage. Folding doors under a fan-light contained the lock now in the Stag parlour. The statue of Rousseau stood under the dark solemn bookcases that surrounded the room—globes, electrifying machines, portfolios about it. In the midst of all this the beautiful Duchess had her writing-table, which displayed what Sheridan called organized disorder. The shape of the room, owing to the semicircular projection of the walls,

*So called because it is below the Plough Room, originally named on a Plough Monday.

made it difficult to adapt a regular form within, which had been done; but
somehow the room is not a pleasant one: hard to say why: it is not haunted;
I wish it were, but something of the Den hangs about it still.

The Bachelor Duke's charming 'morning room' is a bathroom and
cupboards. The Den is Amanda's and Sto's bedroom. Facing north and
of a most curious shape, it is not a good room, but they have never
complained. Its advantage is being next to where their children sleep.

My Sitting-Room (The Boudoir)•

A convenient mezzanine has given space for servant's room and presses above.
To describe an old bachelor's kennel is idle—yet look at the portière made of
a Capuchin's dress given me at Palermo by friend Duke Serra di Falco; at
the Gastein water-jug, and the green pitchers, in which the poorest class
carries water about the streets of Constantinople.

My first memory of this room is of Granny's ubiquitous sad dun-coloured
dirty cotton hangings of a vaguely Chinese look. It was during the war,
when it was the headmistress's study. On the plans it is called the
Boudoir, which means a room for sulking in. It would be difficult to sulk
for long in here, such is the charm of its atmosphere, the things in it and
the views from the windows.

The Bachelor Duke made two rooms out of one by lowering the
ceiling, and putting a little staircase to reach the mezzanine above. The
result is a small sitting-room where the ceiling is the normal height for a
ceiling and a relief from the lofty drawing-room.

In 1959 it was hung with dark green pleated watered silk, bound by a
narrow gilt fillet I found in the granary, that Aladdin's cave of a store
room over the stables. The curtains are of the same green silk, and the
paintwork from dado to floor, windows and ceilings, is dead white—out
of fashion, I know, but it still pleases me as much as it did twenty years
ago.

With all this green and white there is more than ever the need for the
coup de rouge—is that a real expression or did I invent it? Anyway, the
dash of red which somehow pulls a room together. It is provided here by

the red leather drawers of a pair of wellingtons, nineteenth-century filing cabinets, stuffed with letters from sisters, children and friends which some unlucky person will have to sort out or throw away when I am dead.

There are two bookcases, one made in the old doorway to the next room, full of books on goats and cooking, poultry and poetry, gardening and architecture, never opened but having a comforting presence. The one I prize most is *The Life of Ronald Knox* by Evelyn Waugh. Evelyn used to send me his books as they came out, which was very nice of him, as he knew I never read them. He wrote inside *Ronald Knox*, 'For Darling Debo, with love from Evelyn. You will not find a word in this to offend your Protestant sympathies.' I would not have looked any further, but a friend who was in the room when I opened the parcel flipped through the pages and found they were all blank. The perfect present for the non-reader. Another precious book is Primrose O'Connell's *Agricultural Note Book* left to me in his will by Conrad Russell. It is a mine of pre-EEC information of chains and roods, bushels and pecks, scores and hundredweights, which read like poetry in a strange language, just familiar enough to strike the chords of memory.

The furniture is English, small and beautiful, mostly pieces from Compton Place. Sitting at the writing-table you look through a tiny opening cut through the north wall, which is one pane of a blank window outside. The view thus framed of the central entrance arch of the lodge, the park beyond and the craggy top of Froggatt Edge, is like a glimpse of landscape in a Florentine painting.

Being in this room on a winter night, alone or with one or two great friends, the sparkling coal fire with its low brass-bound nursery fender, the familiar things all around, sitting in a chair which becomes a nest with letters and papers and baskets and telephone scattered on the floor, dogs comfortably settled by the fire, or near the draught of the door according to their thickness of coat, is my idea of an evening happily spent.

Not everyone thinks of this room as I do. When Mr Thacker, a highly respected butcher in Bakewell, retired from his business I asked him to tea to say goodbye. We chatted about old times and the war years, when I used to drive a hackney mare into Bakewell to do the meagre shopping and tied her up near the Rutland Arms while I went to see what could be found to eat.

I always called on Mr Thacker whether it was meat ration day or not, hoping to pick up odds and ends for the dogs, and so we became friends. I was curious to know how his business worked, so I asked him to describe what happened after he bought the beasts at the market.

He put down his tea-cup and gazed round the room, taking in the pleated green silk walls, the Velasquez lady with her huge brown eyes and grand Spanish dress, the Zoffany of the Fourth Duke's children in the garden at Chiswick, the Tillemans racehorses, the Meissen dogs and elephants, the Downman watercolours and the Aubusson rugs, and said, 'Well, . . . say *this* was the slaughterhouse . . .'

There are three pictures in this room I must mention. One is a drawing by Boldini of my mother's foot in her 1903 shoe resting on the deck of her father's ketch which was their summer home. One is a self-portrait by Lucian Freud, which he gave to me when I sat to him, painted when he was in hospital in 1942, a kingcup on his eiderdown, a nurse with folded hands and a row of beds behind. And the other is an exquisite tiny Samuel Palmer watercolour of a magic imagined hilly view of cornfields and trees. This lovely little thing came up for auction in Glasgow years before his work was high fashion, and I longed to have it. I left a bid which I thought was sure to succeed, but alas it fetched many times that sum, so I took the illustration from the catalogue, had it framed, and I gaze at it every day.

Andrew's Bedroom (The Duchess's Dressing-Room)•

Our Mother's dressing-room is much altered, but the ceiling remains in the old divisions, with medallions in the style of Angelica Kauffman. There were smaller ones round the frieze, that not only looked like the twelve Caesars, but like several dozen of them: they are gone, and are no loss; but a much-regretted profile in oil, on the fluor spar medallion upon the chimneypiece, was rubbed out inadvertently, when it might have been repaired. A French paper, handsome in its way, has replaced the tattered silk hangings.

The ceiling and chimney-piece remain, the dark green wallpaper and yellow curtains are new. The pictures are all Andrew's, drawings by

A wall in my sitting-room: 'Say *this* was the slaughter-house'

Henry Lamb of me, and Emma at eighteen months, a dusty French street by Lepine, a drawing by Max Beerbohm of 'Lord Londonderry and Lord Curzon explaining to the Duke of Devonshire a joke of Mr Gosse's', old Victor standing with his hands behind his back uncomprehending of what the others are trying hard to make him understand.

The chest-of-drawers is stuffed with ties belonging to the organisations Andrew is interested in. As he is colour-blind he has to be inspected before going out, as he once went to the Game Fair (who gave him their tie the day before) wearing that of the Conservative Friends of Israel. It does not do to turn up at the Annual General Meeting of the British Legion in the All-England Tennis Club tie, or to arrive at the dinner of the Coldstreamers Association dressed as a Buxton Fly-Fisher.

My Bedroom (The Duke's Bedroom)•

The next room to it was my Father's bed-room, exposed to the noise and shaking of the narrowest of passages, that backed the thinnest of partitions behind it.

Here slept he, and when informed that the house was on fire, turned round to sleep on his other side, observing that they had better try to put it out. Am I wrong to record such anecdotes as these? No—for it gives me an opportunity to add, that such apparent apathy was only on the surface of the most generous and noble feelings that could exist—feelings that made him reply to Mr. Heaton, the old and crabbed auditor, when he said, "My Lord Duke, I am very sorry to inform your Grace that Lord Hartington appears disposed to spend a great deal of money."—"So much the better Mr. Heaton; he will have a great deal to spend." Sir Robert Adair, in a sketch of my Father's character, says that his goodness was a deliberate resolution of the mind, grounded on a love of justice. Fox said he preferred his judgment to that of any one; and another person wrote, "he had apprehension, judgment, and perspicuity in their very highest degrees: his ideas were rapid, and took unforseen directions."

It was blue when I first knew it, with Granny's old paper on the walls, as my mother-in-law did not change it in the short time she lived here.

The paper was peeling, and the paint the inevitable dreary beige. All of that was easily changed, of course, but what needed more skill and thought was breaking through the wall to make a tiny bathroom. The Centre rooms already had a bathroom, made in the old passage behind, cold and high, so we divided it in half, lowered the ceiling, and just managed to make two. A jib door was so cleverly made you hardly notice it. The bath is in the recess of a window in the old wall into the courtyard and the wash-basin is set in the marble of an old wash-stand like several others in new bathrooms. This left Granny's bathroom to become a cupboard for Andrew's clothes, of which he has a great many. I asked Mrs Bater, whose husband had been Duke Victor's valet, where he kept his clothes. She looked surprised at the question and said he only had two suits.

I put blue slub silk on the walls of my room, partly because I always thought of the room as blue and partly to go with the bed, whose canopy is lined in blue.

The curtains and bed-hangings are made of a chintz which I have never seen anywhere else—pretty but unremarkable flowers on a white ground with a grand and beautiful border of flamboyant peonies and chrysanthemums. This chintz is repeated in the Scots Bed- and Dressing-Room upstairs and typical of Chatsworth in scale and quality.

Except for the bed, some beautiful chairs from Chiswick, the delicate gilt fillet (the prettiest in the house), which I moved from the Green Satin Bedroom upstairs, and the splendid rococo gilt frame which now holds a mirror (and I am dashed if I can remember what picture was in it) the contents of the room have been bought or borrowed by or given to me.

The four Epstein drawings of his son, aged about three, are powerful and memorable. The first I had was used as a pusher for coal on the floor of his bed-studio by Lucian Freud when I was sitting to him. 'If I get you a shovel which will work better, can I have that drawing?' I do not know if I ever got the shovel, but he gave me the drawing, and I found the others at various auctions. Duncan Grant's picture of the Lower Garden at Lismore is hung too high to see Mrs Hammersley in the shadow of the Irish yew, but she is there all right, wrapped in shawls as usual. A portrait of Sto aged seventeen by Derek Hill is exactly like he was at that age, a George Clausen of potato-diggers by a dying bonfire, a Bevan cart-horse, two Landseers which belong to the house, some

Helleus of my mother, two really bad sentimental water-colours which do not compare with two more by Helen Allingham, a sheep by Rosa Bonheur ('If that were my sheep I'd send for the vet,' Toby Tennant said when it was unwrapped one Christmas morning) and a lot of undistinguished loved objects make up this room, with its glorious view out of one big window.

The Burlington Corridor•

Pursuing now our inspection of the house, you must come with me along the gallery, remarking that it did not exist in the days of our youth. "But how did we get round, looking into the court, before?" Most intelligent, there was a passage, but so very shallow, (the landing of the West staircase formed part of it) passing through the end of the centre room, and so near and close to the back of our parents' apartment, that an immense improvement was wrought by laying down a very thick rug-carpet in the passage, to deaden the sound of the tramping wayfarers.

The walls of this much frequented passage, which leads from our rooms to the Drawing-Room and Dining-Room, are hung with dark brown linen, which I think is the best background for drawings and water-colours. They can hang safely here because there is little direct light. The big cupboard was filled with china arranged by Ilona Solymossy, and I have never wished to change it. The chairs and writing-tables by Kent and the beautiful mirrors with owls peering out, which are mates of the tables, were at Devonshire House.

Andrew bought the Russian urns made of Siberian jasper, and they look very much at home here. I found the Kent torchères in the servants' hall at Compton Place, stained in Victorian fashion, now gilt and restored to their former glory. They are shown in the Hunt water-colour of a Chiswick interior, painted in 1828.

The two Samuel Palmer water-colours, *The Bellman* and *Morning*, were bought by Andrew at the height of the 'Keating forgeries' scandal. *The Bellman* is dark and infinitely peaceful with sleeping cattle, a slow walker on a rutted village road and a late evening sky. *Morning* is dangerously sunny and shows a woman with a pot on her head, a sure sign of 'abroad', which I don't like. *The Bellman* wins hands down.

Keystone on the steps of the south front 'as like as if it had been intended
for my sister Unity'

Looking through the Yellow Drawing-Room to the Dining-Room

The Centre Dressing-Room•

In the centre dressing-room there is a curious drapery of Chinese silk, red within and green without, and yet of one woof. I got it at Moscow, smuggled through the fair of Nijney Novgorod.

The wallpaper, flock, gold, brown and some dark blue, was copied from a fragment found in the closet of the Red Velvet Room. Cole's of Mortimer Street made a great success of it, as they always do with special orders like this. It looks grand, and unique, which is what it is.

The Bachelor Duke's green and red satin curtains of one woof are still there, faded by the western sun. I love the idea of them being smuggled through the fair of Nizhni Novgorod.

People staying in these rooms have to be warned not to talk loudly in their bathroom, as I can hear every word they say in mine.

The Centre Bedroom•

The Centre Room—a passage formerly like the Sabine room above it; then a billiard-room; then, painted white and Andromeda banished, it became a convenient bed-room, as now.

In my notes of 1959 I wrote 'Ceiling white: walls, etc., washed and one coat only of buff paint put on to match background of satin and curtains.' So overwhelming is the bed and its flower-painted satin covered dome and hangings that it was probably right to calm it all down with walls, pilasters, cornice, the lot, plain buff. The outsize dome, ribbed and with layer upon layer of figured painted satin and extravagantly ruched inside with bows, rosettes, silk ropes and tassels, is finished on top with a flourish of gilded wood in the shape of the warning sign for a school on the roads of my youth—an ice cream on fire. It looks more like an Indian elephant's howdah than the roof of an English bed, and big though this room is, the bed dominates it completely. The satin window curtains, alas, have fallen to bits, and I have replaced them by anonymous affairs which do not compete with the bed curtains. Granny and Maud Baillie, the oldest of the Aunts, painted the flowers on the satin which covers the sofa and chairs. They were extremely talented in this sort of work, and it is completely successful.

Lord Home spent a night in this room when he was Prime Minister. The reason for his unexpected visit was the death of President Kennedy in November 1963. Andrew and I went to the funeral and we were given a lift in the Prime Minister's plane. Had it not been for the intense sadness of the reason for the journey it would have been very entertaining, more like a game of consequences than anything in real life. There were eight of us for dinner in the long empty plane, the Duke of Edinburgh representing the Queen, Mr Harold Wilson, Leader of the Opposition, Mr Jo Grimond, leader of the Liberals, the Homes and ourselves.

On the return journey the company had diminished for various reasons to the Homes, Jo Grimond and me. When we were still over the Atlantic the pilot was told there was thick fog over London Airport and we were diverted to Manchester. I persuaded the passengers to stay the night at Chatsworth instead of in an airport hotel. Messages were sent and the plan made. I knew the house was prepared for guests, as we were expecting a party for the weekend which included Princess Margaret. She was to have the Centre Bedroom. When at last we arrived, and our cold and hunger had been dealt with I showed Alec into this room. He looked at the enormous bed, turned down and ready, looked back at me and said, 'If I lie very still and don't turn over *you won't have to change the sheets.*'

The Red Velvet Room●

Long live native talent!—here shine, with one or two exceptions, pure British specimens of art.

Sir Thomas Lawrence's George IV. is the second he painted : the first was a full length for Lady Conyngham. This one was actually sent to Rome in 1824, to be presented to Cardinal Consalvi. His death occurring, and not long after that of Elizabeth, Duchess of Devonshire, who was to have had it, the picture came back to London. The King gave it to me in his usual characteristic manner : "Hart, will you do me a favour?" "What is it, sir?" "I wish you to be on the commission for rebuilding Windsor Castle." Hart respectfully declined, and, being in opposition to H. M.'s Ministers, said he had better not. "Well, Hart, you have refused me that; will you do me another favour? will you accept my picture, by Lawrence?"

That is one of a thousand traits that did, do, and will attach me to him and to his memory, while I have breath in my body.

Sir Joshua Reynolds's picture of my Mother, with a child (Lady Carlisle) in her lap, is one of his best, though some people dislike the attitude, and do not allow the likeness. Sir Thomas Lawrence made a wonderful copy of this for the gallery at Windsor Castle: he copied faithfully, but threw in the charm of his own particular colouring.

The Queen and Prince Albert used this room to breakfast in. It was formerly a popular, much inhabited bed-room: it is one of the places that, notwithstanding the total change, revives now, and always must, some singular recollections. I resist the temptation of detailing them to you. I compel the garrulity of age to abstain from spreading itself on paper—and, though it amused me extremely to see Fish Crawford's pillow dressed in a cap and painted like a baby, and to assist in the transaction, it and other adventures would surely not have the same effect upon you and others—so write them not, my pen, the cento memorie e cento, inspired by this room.

My favourite bedroom in the house, except for my own. It has been alternately bedroom and sitting-room, and is once again 'a popular, much inhabited bed-room'. We put a chimneypiece from Devonshire House to replace a plain bolection moulding. The Utrecht velvet on the walls is made of wool and is beloved of moths. The painted bed was moved from the Green Satin Room. Not only the bed is painted, so are the satin curtains, draperies and bedspread, all in a sad state of disintegration, and I thought beyond repair, till I sent them to Lady Meade-Fetherstonhaugh of Uppark in Sussex, who bathed them in saponaria and ran hundreds of threads up and down, giving them all a new lease of life.

The glass chandelier came from the staircase at Compton Place and the flowered chintz-covered chairs and chaise-longue are from a bedroom there.

I bought the pink Aubusson carpet with white doves in the corners with money left me by my brother.* The Liotard and Russell pastels have all

*Tom Mitford, died of wounds in Burma, 1945.

the charm of their medium, and the Rysbracks of Chiswick were already here (but not in this room) when Andrew bought the one of the trees in tubs in the garden there to complete the series.

The bathroom next door was a closet as high as the two rooms it connects. To make it more comfortable as a bathroom the ceiling was lowered and coved so it did not interfere with the big west window. It was painted white and hit you in the eye from the road across the river, a perfectly awful staring stripe of dead white. So we turned it into reflected Derbyshire sky by changing it to dirty blue and green with a lot of black in it, and it has disappeared from view very satisfactorily.

The Tapestry Gallery (The Picture Gallery)•

That you remember the former passage, (replaced by this) I well know: low, full of small windows, the walls white within, and narrow, exceedingly cold, but smelling of spirits of wine, employed to heat the polite Lawton's tea-table—Lawton, groom of the chambers, who succeeded to a snuffy old Frenchman named Beauvais. In course of time, having framed my collection of sketches, I placed them here, and that was my first splash at Chatsworth, and it was much commended. They are now elevated to the upper floor.

The two panels over the doors were in the Music Room, and many think should go there again—a point I cannot decide.

The table on the window side is made of a most beautiful slab—a sort of granite containing large garnets—from Schwerin. When there, I saw one like it being polished for the Landgrave of Hesse, and ordered this, which was sent me for one hundred crowns.

The passage was painted peacock green from floor to ceiling by Granny Evie after the Great War. Before that Louise Duchess preferred it salmon pink. Now it is covered from dado to cornice in blue-green velveteen, which came from Peter Jones and cost £1 a yard. It was hung by Cole of Sheffield, their first attempt at hanging stuff on walls. The Victorian round marble-topped tables, supported by swans, were stored a furlong apart. The tapestries are Lille, *c.* 1730, after designs by Teniers. We brought them here from a bedroom at Hardwick. The set of eight George III chairs, mahogany with gros and petit point needlework seats depicting blue and white Chinese teapots, came from the same treasure house.

The big mirrors on the walls are from Chiswick, a collection of large minerals on window sills and floor were acquired by Andrew, as were most of the illustrated books. Here is the drink tray and the visitor's book, and here for many years was the notice of 1841 which read, 'In wet and dirty weather parties of no more than 8 persons may see the principal apartments.' A few years ago this notice was removed to a Safe Place and is, of course, lost.

The Blue Drawing-Room (The Music Room)•

To make this room, the Chapel Bedchamber and another chamber were united soon after my Father's marriage in 1774. A sort of white tabbinet lined the walls. Sir Joshua's picture of my Mother with a child was framed

The fender in the Blue Drawing-Room

Curtains, carved swags, gilt vellum bows, Carr of York's cornice and Victorian roses all mixed up in the Blue Drawing-Room

into the top of a looking-glass. A jib door opened to the passage. It was a gay pretty room.

As to me, I was obliged to re-embellish what was decayed, but could not equal it; and, after covering the walls with cut velvet, that I imagined was perfection, a year's experience obliged me to strip it off, and to convert it into curtains both for this room and for the library, where it succeeds most entirely. The blue silk from Lyons replaces it here without offence.

The ceiling is bad and apt to crack: it ought to have been replaced by a new one. It has been enlivened by garlands of roses, and an accidental thought caused them to remain with the flowers not gilt, which has a good effect.

The chimneypiece is a new purchase, ugly enough, bought in a hurry, and tolerated only because the roses thereon agree with the ceiling. The frame above it is made of old fragments by Gibbons, found in the store-room here. I beg you to admire the fender: it was bought for me by Mr. Ridgway at I know not what London sale. The fender looks as if it were listening to Mendelssohn's "Midsummer Night's Dream."

This used to be the most joyous and frequented of all the rooms at Chatsworth. The solemnities of my band may make it less so now, but to me it is more enjoyable, and when the young want to dance, they migrate to the velvet room and gallery, which suffice for a small party.

When I first knew the house and we used to drive over in a pony cart from Churchdale or The Rookery at Ashford, and later came across the park from Edensor House, this room had thin beige velveteen curtains which neither met in the middle nor reached the floor. The remnants of pale blue silk hung in tatters on the walls with lumps of grubby cotton wool sticking out. The ceiling, cornice and dado were painted Granny's favourite deep cream. She took away two bird's eye maple doors 'which had no relation to anything else in this part of the house' and made the jib door into the passage. It was the schoolroom of the Aunts, and Granny liked sitting here because there was nothing which could get spoilt — it was for children and their dogs, and the furniture was far from what she called 'important'. It was the meeting-place of young and old, welcoming, light, shabby and cheerful as it is to this day.

My mother-in-law found two huge rolls of new blue silk in a windowless recess in the attics when looking for nothing in particular, the same silk as the rotten stuff, ordered and put away by Louise Duchess.

She hung it in 1950, and it transformed the room and remains good thirty years later, though faded to a silvery colour, which makes people wonder why it is called the *Blue* Drawing-Room. There is not enough silk to cover all the walls, so there must always be very big pictures in the middle of the east and west walls and over the fireplace to hide the gaps.

I found an empty frame lying on its side in a far attic passage which is nearly the right size for the fireplace gap, and put a looking-glass in it. I know not what picture came out of this frame. You can just see the plain material at its sides.

My mother-in-law rescued the half-moon tables under the looking glasses between the windows from the stony North Entrance Hall, where they must have looked very out of place, and was intrigued to discover her instinct in putting them here was right, as they fit exactly because they were made for the place.

I was stuck for curtains in this room, and asked Mr Maltby for advice. Maltby (1881–1966) was house carpenter from 1910 and knew as much about the contents of the house as anyone. He said, 'There are wooden swags which belong to these windows. The Dowager didn't like them and took them away.' I could not imagine what he meant, but he went off and came back, bearing the said carved swags which were covered in the cut velvet the Bachelor Duke put on the walls and did not like — proof that they were here before 1840. We stripped them of the velvet (which

Lady Caroline Lamb (1785–1828) by Thomas Phillips

Georgiana Spencer Duchess of Devonshire, sketch by Sir Joshua Reynolds

The Acheson Sisters, granddaughters of Louise Duchess by her first marriage, by J. S. Sargent

no longer went with anything in the room), and painted gold with the white cotton festoon blinds they make a proper finish to the tops of the windows.

Granny very much disliked everything of the nineteenth century, it was too close to her time, and she despised it as people of my generation despise the work of the fashionable decorators of the 1920s. But she did not destroy these things. They were put away to be re-discovered and fitted into the jigsaw once more. In this case she was wrong in thinking them to be nineteenth-century. It is now known that Carr of York worked in this room for the Fifth Duke when he was building the splendid Crescent in Buxton. Much of the embellishment including the sham draperies of the windows, their tables, and some of the cornice and dado is of this time.

The three different dates of decoration, seventeenth century, late eighteenth and mid-nineteenth, shake down together so well in the two drawing-rooms that the mixture might have been intended.

The void between the double doors leading into the chapel gallery was the place chosen by Andrew for the television, an object of great hideosity and better hidden except for the rare occasions when it is wanted.

Mostly English pictures are hung here, dominated by Sir Joshua Reynolds' portrait of Georgiana and her baby, a charming sketch of the

Myself, Andrew and Elizabeth Cavendish by Lucian Freud

same Duchess by the same artist and his portrait of Lady Elizabeth
Foster looking distinctly sly. The big picture of Georgiana flying
through a cloud by Mrs Cosway (wife of the miniaturist) is the one
which reminded her son, the Bachelor, most of her. Lady Caroline
Lamb dressed as a footman, by Phillips, is next, her pert and irritating
face turned sideways, and on the opposite wall is the cheerful Sargent of
the Acheson sisters, granddaughters of the Duchess of Manchester who
later married the Eighth Duke of Devonshire. I love this picture, but
question whether the girls could ever have been so tall and thin. Never
mind, it is a wholly pleasing affair, and I am glad the repeated offers of
American museums to buy it have been refused. The Sargent is yet
another example of rapid change in taste. Granny could not find a place
for it (which meant she did not like it) and lent it to the Tate where it
reposed underground. Writing in 1950 she suggested it should be sold
'when back in fashion'. No, thanks.

Round, and even on, the jib door into the passage is a collection of
family portraits by Lucian Freud. They are of my mother-in-law,
Andrew, his sisters Elizabeth Cavendish and Anne Tree, my son and
myself. The one of me was on the public route of the house for a time.
Someone heard an old lady say to her friend, 'That's the Dowager
Duchess. It was taken the year she died.' I was thirty-four when it was
painted, but the old lady had a point; the face is sadly raddled, and a pale
green moustache covers the upper lip. There is no doubt that I get more
like the painting every year. Lucian's portrait of Elizabeth is the best to
my mind, with Anne a close second.

I bought the tall red sofa from Colefax & Fowler, who got it from the Kimbolton sale. The needlework panels on the cushions were pelmets from an attic bedroom at Compton Place. Miss Feeney stitched them on the cushions. The round library table and the books in it were Georgiana's.

I bought the pair of bronze and ormolu urns in the King's Road soon after the war for £20.

The Blue Drawing-Room, with the incomparable view south over Cibber's sea-horse fountain to the Emperor Fountain in the canal beyond, is again the 'most joyous and frequented room' in the house.

The Yellow Drawing-Room•

More Indian silk, yellow, bought at the Custom House at the same time as the red. I added here the deep frieze to the cornice, and enriched the corners of the ceiling.

The walls are still covered by the Bachelor Duke's yellow Indian silk, much patched, and the curtains are made of the same stuff. The furniture was put back more or less as I believe it was before the war, including the Chiswick bookcases and the flowery Axminster carpet with tulips and roses, which was at Devonshire House. The pair of *verre eglomisé* looking-glasses used to be in the Centre Bedroom, but I think they go very well here. The red in the surrounds picks up the red of the roses in the silk. The chairs, footstools and sofas and some tables are by François Hervé, commissioned by Georgiana and the Fifth Duke in the 1780s, and the pier glass tops by another Frenchman, Gaubert.

There was no piano in the house when we came here, only an ancient pianola in the School Room. Michael Astor noticed this lack in 1959 when he stayed here the first time we had friends for the weekend. He said, 'I'm going to get a piano for my house when I go to London next week, so I'll get one for you as well.' And with typical Astor generosity, he did so. A lot of jolly music has been thumped out of it since then, and I always feel grateful to Michael for such a magnificent present.

On it sits the bronze head of Sophy aged two by Epstein, finished

On the piano in the Yellow Drawing-Room

three weeks before he died, and the Meissen models of the Empress of Russia's dog, a good old mongrel on a grand china cushion.

The Dining-Room (The Drawing-Room)•

You have had the patience to follow me thus far without touching the offices, which may be done hereafter.

I like my task; but at times it turns upon me, and I feel exceedingly ridiculous, and like an auctioneer when he makes his inventory, and puts the striking features into capital letters.

The Drawing-Room was the Dining-Room. The woodwork round it, in its unexampled irregularity, was originally as you see it now. The chimney stands between a fat panel and a lean one: the fireplace, not being in the centre, might at least have been opposite the central window of the three it looks at, but it is not. The doors are not in a line with their opposite windows; neither do they approach equally the ends of the room, as you will perceive, if you remark the narrow panel to the right of the library-door.

With proportions thus arranged, I found the room with a plain

123

whitewashed ceiling unfit to be retained. The question was, what kind of ceiling to adapt to the wainscot, which I was desirous of preserving. Sir Jeffry Wyatville solved this difficulty by the design of a ceiling, which, by having its centre in a line with the middle window, and margins of different widths, would do, whatever changes might be made in the panelling of the room, and equally well without any change; and thus, although the windows themselves err as much as their corresponding doors, he has contrived to satisfy the eyes of all men.

Naked and bare was the room; the two outer mouldings of the panels, of handsome work, enclose dreary spaces of wood, painted white. The panels over the doors, retained by me for old acquaintance sake, were the work of Reinagle, father of the Reinagles who have painted in my time. The dog with an intelligent head is said by tradition to have been a notorious thief of strawberries.

The floor was matted like the floors at Hardwick. Six pale slabs of grey Ashford, with taper white legs, surrounded the room: four of them have been made into dressing-tables, but, if you like to see them in their primitive state, two now adorn the steward's room.

A huge silver dish (called Cellini, of course) stood on one of them against the wall, alone contending against the dreary, washy appearance of everything else. Here, however, for years the course of hospitality ran—the public days' repasts. Here dined Garrick, and Madame Mara sang.

Here, in my time, while the library was rebuilt and restored, deal shelves up to the ceiling, that pervaded not only this but the drawing-room and music-room, held volume upon volume, dingy, unwiped, unbound; but they imparted no gloom: For a long time, Lawrence's portrait of George IV. was placed, backed always by books, at the West end, and so lit up at night by shaded lamps, that it was an illusion, and the truly loyal would hardly sit down in his presence.

Here were acted numerous charades: sometimes their theatrical curtain remained suspended over the table at which we dined.

Here dined with me the Grand Duke Nicolas. The Princess Victoria's charade of Kenilworth happened after the books had been replaced in the library, but before the other changes: the date of that was 1832, her first visit.

Then came the want of decoration; portraits, full lengths, above all, were put in requisition. Mary Queen of Scots, and Charles I., from Chiswick; Henry VIII., and Philip II., General Monk, and two Tintorets from Devonshire House, were pressed into the service, but they were all of different

Myself in the Dining-Room with Stout, best of dogs

sizes—an objection overruled by me, who suggested the filling-up of the panels with Oncidium Lanceanum, and O. Cavendishianum, so that short and long are allowed at the same glance, and the irregularity only accords with the other numerous deviations of the room. An inner moulding carved in wood, of Oncidium Lancifolium, was added to the frames.

It was necessary here, as in several parts of the house, to place strong iron girders in the ceiling, to support the sinking floor of the State Rooms above.

The furniture is old, and belonged to the middle drawing-room; and the couches, formal there when close to the wall, form agreeable groups in their new place.

Bartolini's copy of the Venus de Medicis is placed in a circular couch: the hands of the statue are slightly varied from the original. There sat Queen Victoria to see the illumination of the fountains and pleasure-ground in December, 1843.

The two yellow marble columns were brought from the ruins of Carthage by Sir Augustus Clifford. The birds were collected by Gibson, the gardener whom I sent to India.

The Curtains, here as well as in the dining-room, are made of Indian silk. He who has to furnish a great house is embarked in a sea of trouble, and nothing but experience can teach what ought to be done—except Mr. John Crace, who, I have latterly found, can teach it still better. The curtains were first of all put up in the Library, where, with their heavy cornices, they were disapproved of and condemned. The Dining-Room accepted them: the Drawing-Room would only have the drapery, and the rest of the cornices went to Devonshire House.

The Duchess of Sutherland ordered the carpet the same for the three Drawing Rooms. The chairs are covered with an imitation in English silk of the cut velvet ordered by me at Genoa.

The Dining-Room was the Drawing-Room. The Bachelor Duke's and Wyatville's masterly treatment of it remained, but the whole was dingy and dreary in the extreme when we first had charge of it. The paint was dark cream colour, and two of the windows were nearly blocked up by huge urns that have since returned to Chiswick where they belonged.

We painted it in three shades of grey and washed the thick gold of the Victorian ceiling with Lux.

The difficulty was how to get the food to this room from the kitchen below. We finally decided to put a lift in the old stairwell, which sticks out on the east side of the house. A hole was knocked through the wall (as the old stairs had opened into the library next door) and for months the great stones from Bess's house lay in dusty heaps on the floor.

The picture by Lely of General Monk was in the way of the entrance to the new lift, as it was fitted in one of the Bachelor Duke's ornate frames on the wall where the jib door had to go. What to do, but cut it in half so when the door is opened the old soldier's legs swing round, startling the diners. The jib door was most skilfully made and when it is shut General Monk appears complete, legs and all.

The dining-table is from Devonshire House, and so are the chairs. The curtains are the ones put by the Bachelor Duke, relined, the braid unpicked and resewn on to new red satin by the patient Miss Feeney, who has done so much restoration and new work in the house. The Duchess of Sutherland's carpet is still here but in a sad state and full of holes.

The wonderful bluejohn urn used to be on the banister at the foot of the main staircase and was moved here by Andrew. He had it lit from inside by an electric bulb which looked beautiful but worried a bluejohn fancier because of the danger of damage by heat, so Andrew asked Professor Haszeldine of the University of Manchester Institute of Science and Technology to look at it, and he produced a special bulb which lights it but is hardly warm.

The pictures are unchanged, fitted into their frames of orchids in lattice so cleverly invented by the Bachelor Duke and Wyatville among the other enrichments which take the eye from the irregularities of the room. Some of the frames, damaged and in need of new gold, were painted in 1958 instead of being done properly with gold leaf. Dear good John Fowler (who never worked here but came to stay several times when I carried his patterns round Sudbury Hall after the National Trust took it over in 1967) used to go very close to this awful paint, push up his spectacles and gaze long and carefully at it. He never said anything, but the pitying look he gave when eventually he turned away was quite enough for me to know how badly he thought I'd done by these frames.

John was the prince of decorators, a scholar with a wonderful memory for whole rooms and the smallest details, and the best appreciator of beautiful places and things I have ever known. He had a clever way of making sure the right stuff of the right colour was chosen for covering furniture and making curtains for a National Trust house where a committee was meant to do the choosing. Knowing that he was the one who knew, he was determined, rightly, to make the decisions, and he bowed to the committee system like this; he produced several patterns and laid them out side by side. Picking up the first he said, 'I expect you think that is too pale,' the second, 'I'm sure you think that blue is not right for the date' and the third, which he had already chosen, he would grasp in his hand and say with a note of triumph in his voice, 'And *you* darling, *you*, with your *unerring eye*, will say this one is *perfect*.'

But that is nothing to do with the Dining-Room, and we must go back and look at the Berlin china plates and dishes which stand on the marble-topped tables. They are part of a large service of two hundred pieces, including china handled knives and forks, bought by an ancestor of mine from Warren Hastings when that unlucky man's possessions were sold to pay for his trial. My mother used this service for supper at the dances she gave for my sisters and myself. No doubt some was broken, but it is still a remarkable set. My father, who had a passion for selling things, sent them to Sotheby's in 1948, and I persuaded Andrew to buy them. The whole service cost £410. The next day there was a piece in the *Daily Telegraph* headed 'Lord Hartington pays top price at Sotheby's' and we were afraid his father would see it and be cross at such extravagance. I suppose it was the bargain of a lifetime.

The bronze of Park Top, Andrew's great race mare, is by Angela Conner. Near it are the King George VI and Queen Elizabeth Cup, the Coronation Cup and la Coupe de Longchamp, all won by this much-loved mare.

To return to the public route we go back to the Great Staircase.

Beyond the Staircase, and sometimes open, are the Scots and Leicester Rooms.

The Queen of Scots and Leicester Rooms '

Queen of Scots' Rooms. The space taken up by these two rooms, by the broad passage of communication, and the vestibule at the top of the great stairs, was occupied by two very large rooms and a closet, called the Queen of Scots' apartment. There was nothing remarkable about them, except the tradition that they had been preserved, propped up, and built round, from the old house. They were in the style of the State Rooms, but very inferior, and with plain white ceilings: the great want of lodging room here caused their alteration. The account-books in my possession prove, that the woodwork and mouldings were made more than a hundred years after the death of Mary. I find in the accounts of September 5, 1693—

The Alcove Room in the Scots and Leicesters

The coronation chairs of King William IV and Queen Adelaide

Alcove
Bedroom

Alcove
Lobby

Leicester
Bedroom

Wellington
Dr'ng
Room Bedroom

Dr'g
R'm

Green
Satin
Bedroom

State
Dining
Room

Scots Passage

Scots
Bedroom

Scots
Dressing
Room

Scots
Lobby

Great
Stairs

State
Drawing
Room

State
Music
Room

South Sketch Gallery

State
Bedroom

West Sketch Gallery

PUBLIC ROUTE
SECOND FLOOR

Stairs

Red
Room
West

China
Closet

State
Dr'ss'g
Room

"Received then of James Wildon, by my Lord's especial order, to buy wainscoat boards to be sent down to Chatsworth to finish the Queen of Scots' apartment, and for the Gallery, the sum of £100. I say, received the same sum.

"Henry Lobb."

There was nothing, therefore, to lament in their destruction, and the gain is immense in accommodation, and free access to so many apartments. Even the red velvet bed, called the state bed of Mary Stuart, had ducal coronets at its feet; the looking-glass had them also, so that the eye could not dwell on anything with certainty as having been seen by her.

The Alcove Room is convenient, but cold in winter: the winds of the North seem to penetrate the thickness of the walls.

The Leicester Rooms, bed-room and dressing-room, are handsome and richly furnished.

129

The Wellington Room contains a bed that came down for the Queen, but I rejected it for her apartment, and the great Duke first slept in it here.

The Green Silk Room. Here is the Queen's bed, which was removed to a room downstairs when she came. Once I took to this room for my summer, or rather autumn, sitting-room, and wrote from Danieli's, at Venice, to have the door opened to the State Room, from the great enjoyment of sunshine in the south-east corner of that quondam palazzo. The housekeeper's despair at another wall broken through! More dirt, and dust, and litter! It was done and inhabited: the sun alone was disobedient, and now the room has relapsed into dormitory.

We did not plan to do up these rooms, but when most of the house was finished and clean they seemed sadly neglected, so once again, in November 1965, we started on a new bit of house.

There are seven bedrooms here, two face into the courtyard and five look east over the garden. Till the war they were the nearly best visitors' rooms (the best were the Centres), yet there was only one bath and lavatory between the lot of them, and that was in a cupboard in the passage over the Oak Stairs.

One of the Scots, the two Leicesters and the Wellington have beautiful Chinese wallpaper, and in the Wellington the banana *Musa cavendishii* is portrayed almost life-size. In Granny's day the bed was against this wall (the bells for Maid and Valet indicate the place) and she used to say she thought the banana was somewhere in the paper but that it was a myth. She never saw it till the bed was moved.

The Solymossy sisters made all the green and silver silk hangings for the domed bed in here from extra curtains which had no place. The vast bed in the first Leicester bedroom used to have a giant dome and curtains. Granny had an idea that the resulting lack of air gave its occupants sore throats, so it was banished to the granary where its sad skeleton remains.

The Green Satin Bedroom is no longer green satin or a bedroom. I took the painted bed downstairs to the Red Velvet, so this room has become a sort of false drawing-room. The green satin on the walls was quite rotted away, and I replaced it with a colourless paper, and hung portraits of Lord and Lady Burlington and William Kent. The furniture covered in Fulham tapestry went to Christie's when death duties had to be raised in the fifties but did not fetch its reserve. I was glad to see it come home again, and it looks at ease here. The oyster cabinet was at Compton Place. It suffered from the wild birth-pangs of the central heating when it was first installed and is badly cracked.

The Green Satin Dressing-Room still has the stuff on the wall from which it gets its name, but it is in very poor condition. The frame of the triple mirror over the fireplace once had a nobler role as it was a spare for the Memling triptych, now in the National Gallery.

In the lobby are the enormous coronation chairs of William IV and Queen Adelaide, which the Bachelor Duke had such difficulty in getting,* more like props for a pantomime than pieces of furniture for humans to sit on.

We have never used these rooms, but I am glad they were done up and made presentable, as they are the only bedrooms in the open part of the house (except the State Bedroom, which I do not count because of its gloomy grandeur). The Chinese papers and some of their hangings are very pretty indeed, and it would be sad if they could not be seen.

The State Dining-Room○

It was never dined in, that I know of—the first room of this great unappropriated apartment, which consumes in useless display the best habitable part of the house. What bed-rooms might have been made here, with the South sun, and beautiful views! I was much tempted, but finished conservatively by repairing the sinking floors and threatening ceilings; and, as a museum of old furniture, and a walk in bad weather, I am well contented to retain this dismal ponderous range of Hampton Court-like chambers.

Gibbon is generally believed to have been the carver employed here. Whoever carved, his triumph is in this first room: the game, fish, and fruit, over the chimneypiece, are perfection. I hope to find Gibbon's receipts, or some proof of his having served, but at present there is none; and Mr. Ashton, who was Sir Jeffry's foreman, and succeeded him, has sent me a most curious collection of papers, formerly entrusted to Sir Jeffry, in which I find that Talman, the surveyor or architect, had employed Thomas Young for carving in 1688, and in 1693 Joel Lobb and Samuel Watson, who engaged to

*See State Music-Room, p. 138

Laguerre's portrait
of the housekeeper

finish the carving of the Queen of Scots' apartment, and not to work at the South rooms till that was done; and in 1694 they received "my Lord his Grace's order to buy Limetree, to finish the carving in the great chamber." The oak boards of the floor for the upper story were ordered in 1689.

Talman was employed here as surveyor from 1686 to 1696. He pulled down the old South front in 1687, and the masons and carpenters appear to have been for more than three years engaged in rebuilding it. He undertook to build the East front in 1693. I find the most formal articles signed between "the Right Honourable William Earl of Devonshire, Lord Steward of their Majesties Household, and W. Talman of the parish of St. James, within the liberties of Westminster, in the County of Middlesex, Gentleman." Still I believe that Talman was a Frenchman. During the ten years he did not pass more than four and twenty weeks here, and his diet during that time cost £29.

The ceilings, twice restored by me, are beginning, to my sorrow, to crack again. Mrs. Hacket, the angry housekeeper, is uninjured: she was immortalized by Verrio as a Fury cutting the thread of Fate. I find her named as housekeeper in 1689.

Antonio Verrio painted here in 1691–2. He received £550. Laguerre, and his assistant Ricard, had £438; but they were employed from January 1688 to the end of 1692. You must find all these dates very tiresome, indulgent sister. The painters have left no sign of which part was confided to each: on the whole, their works are satisfactory, and while

132

The State Dining-Room

> *On painted ceilings you devoutly stare,*
> *Where sprawl the works of Verrio and Laguerre,*

you do not, like Pope, condemn them.

    The papers thus returned to me had a memorandum of Sir Jeffry's upon them—"1837. To be punctually and carefully returned to the Duke." You are the cause of my obtaining them, and at the same time the sketches and drawings of the alterations here, which will form a most interesting folio series, full of the cleverest designs and ideas, and also the regretted architect's sketch-book of his first impressions on arriving. You are the cause, because, on writing to you, I was led to have inquiries made of Mr. Ashton, which produced this tardy, but most liberal, concession of what certainly ought to belong to me.

    Campbell's bust of the Princess Pauline, much better than his statue, has almost become Lady Newburgh: placed opposite to the same sculptor's bust of my poor friend, all the world will have it that it is she, and is welcome to think so—though, to be sure, it is rather like comparing heaven to earth, which is said without the slightest disrespect to that element departed. You see here something of the feature that used to make her brother for ever say to her "Tais toi, avec ton petit nez pointu."

Here is the top of the Wanstead table. The green China vases were bought at Watson Taylor's sale for £72. After the peace in 1814 there came a rage for collecting and repairing the old furniture called Buhl: cabinets, tables, and pedestals were sold at enormous prices, and some fortunate people found their garrets full of the commodity, rejected by the changes of fashion in decoration. One of these tables was found here, another in a lumber-room at Chiswick, and another was bought for me by a lady as a wonderful bargain at £140. They are, after all, a disagreeable possession; beautiful when newly furbished up, but apt to soil, and to get broken, from parts of the inlaid work that will start, however discreetly rubbed. I have done with collecting Buhl goods.

The model of Grassington mine, given by the mineral Captain Eady, is the cleverest, best piece of mechanical imitation I ever saw, entirely absolving me from any necessity of going to look at my subterranean property in the bowels of the earth.

I must not forget the old cabinet with glass doors, found at Burlington House; instead of Buhl, it looked like coarse black wood, but came out beautiful and gay on being cleaned. It seemed to have been used by the Duke of Portland, who, with his family, passed so many years there. A curious state of things: he married my Aunt, and after her death in 1794 never saw my Father, yet continued to live rent-free in that house till he died; nor do I know that there was any difference or coolness to account for the non-intercourse. To attempt relating what the cabinet holds would be vain, for it contains all things in the world, and some others.

'Dismal and ponderous' the Bachelor Duke says. Too big to relate to real life, too high and too far away to eat in or use, there are many details of incredible delicacy and beauty in Watson's carvings. The furniture is the best we can show, and the result is a room to walk through and look at or to sit in alone in the low winter sunshine to absorb the details of carving, the furious housekeeper on the ceiling and the views to the east and south.

The vast table in the middle of the room is the hall table from Wanstead, once thought to be by Kent and the biggest he ever made. It had a spare top of Ashford marble which lay for years in a huge crate in the passage near the lamp room and is now in the middle part of the (1970) greenhouse.

Typical of Chatsworth to produce two tops for one immense table.

I agree with the Bachelor Duke in his dislike of Buhl furniture which has left this room and is scattered about the other state rooms. Perhaps it is unsuitable for an English house because of its totally foreign appearance. It always makes me think of the American lady who described her collection of French furniture to me at a dinner party in New York. She got carried away with enthusiasm and said, 'You should see my furniture. It's *so* Louis, why it's *Louis Louis*.' That's what I think about Buhl. Too Louis. Yet other French furniture fits in so well.

The State Drawing-Room°

The ceiling is in better order here: the tapestry is from Raffaelle's cartoons, and has not been altered; it hangs just where, and as, I found it; but some shabby mouldings round it have been removed, and replaced by good ones. The one portrait, an oval in the carved work, is the first Duke, who built this front, and decorated the whole of the interior, and created the garden and the waterworks. The Buhl cabinets are handsome, bought on different occasions in London. The chairs, couches, and screens, of beautiful Beauvais tapestry, were sold to me by Lady Canterbury; and it was more because I could not say "no" in reply to the earnest honest manner, and hearty recommendations of the beautiful Irish woman, than that I wanted them. They were her Lord the Speaker's perquisites, and had been repaired on the occasion of George the Fourth's sleeping at Westminster, the night before his Coronation. They form a suitable handsome decoration here; but vexed was I to find, that an Ex-Speaker and his Lady seemed to look upon the transaction as unjustifiable, and the purchase quite a mistake.

The tapestries were woven at Mortlake *circa* 1635, and the 'goodness' of the Bachelor Duke's mouldings is open to doubt. The lower bits are punctured in a ready-made woodworm way, and the scale of the egg and tongue above is a size too big. Like so much stuff of the 1840s it is just wrong when superimposed on earlier rooms. Nevertheless the tapestries made a grand impression on the upstairs walking tour.

The Coromandel furniture was at Hardwick when I first saw it, but belongs in this house because the pieces from which it is made once lined the walls of the State Dressing-Room. Hardwick was used as a repository for everything that was out of fashion, which is one of the reasons that so much survives which might have been given away or destroyed at the dates when it was not admired.

In Granny's notes of 1950 she writes, 'Rachel used this room till she married.' And adds, surprisingly, 'It was also the home of the jazz band.'

The State Music-Room°

I first saw the French cuir repoussé at Fontainebleau: it suits the old Chateau perfectly, and it does well here, but there is too much gilding and colour employed on it in this room.

There used to be no door to the North, for there was no gallery, or possibility of getting round the house without going through all the State Rooms. The door and doorcase, surmounted by a famous wooden pen, were in the small room at the South-west corner: they used to open into the dressing-room of the red apartment in the West front; and the husbands had to emerge this way, which made Prince Leopold, when conducted to Mr. Abercrombie's room for conversation, remark, and re-mark to him, "You have got a very fine approach to your room."

Chatsworth tradition says that Gibbon made the pen to deceive Verrio, and Verrio the fiddle to deceive Gibbon. The fiddle? Yes, behind the door there—once on the door of some cupboard, and the salient peg assisted in the delusion.

The hangings here were made of green velvet, and eight not very prepossessing full lengths hung upon them. The first Duke had, I am sure, the best reasons for selecting the coterie, but his unworthy descendant does not know, as he would wish, why and wherefore each was chosen—except, let us see, the Duke of Ormond was his father-in-law, the fourth Earl of Bedford was grandfather of his dear friend Lord Russell—the first Duke of Rutland's son married a daughter of the same Lord Russell, and so did his own son; the brave Charles Cavendish was his uncle, Lord Falkland his friend, but why two Earls of Pembroke and the red man were there, questo non so.

Chantrey's bust of George IV. electrified the King's friends while he lived, but now it is not so easy to make them perceive its merits, which appear

Cuir repoussé with the Bachelor Duke's portrait in leather in the top left-hand corner

to me very great—and did so too to sculptor Chantrey, as he charged £210 for it.

Rauch, a famous Prussian, made me the bust of the Emperor Nicolas: he was sent to Rome when very young by the beautiful and unfortunate Queen of Prussia, and was afterwards employed in the unrivalled monument of her in the Tomb of Charlottenberg. The bust is like the Czar: it would be difficult to fail in copying those regular features of the finest head in the world. The head of the Empress is not unlike; it is any how less so than Rauch's bust of her, which is the reason of my having preferred the work of an inferior artist.

Louis XIV could find no other place: he was bought at the Duchesse de Berri's sale at the same time as Granet's picture.

I am unworthy of china, porcelain, &c., but I know that the dragons on *those vases have got five claws, and that it is an immense advantage to them in collectors' eyes.*

The Majesties of William IV. and Adelaide the charitable were crowned in Westminster Abbey in those two chairs. After the ceremony, during which I was Chamberlain, I thought they would, almost of their own accord, drop into the State Rooms here, because their predecessors, that held George III. and the virtuous Charlotte, had stared me in the face here all the days of my life; and that the "Prince of the Whigs" (so called by the King's mother, when he was humbled—qu., honoured?—by being dismissed from Lord Bute's Council) should have permitted the tokens of his servitude to remain here appears to me to have been an exemplary condescension.

However, the chairs did not arrive spontaneously; and really had it not been for the cordial advice of the dear old fat Princess Augusta, I should hardly have encountered the difficulties made to prevent my obtaining them. The official underlings actually got the Queen's chair placed in the House of Lords, under the canopy, as if there was no other to be had for the purpose. Nevertheless, here they are, and in my turn I was turned out myself; and you remember well that it was in good company, with Lords Lansdowne, Holland, Melbourne, &c. When pressed to reassume my place with them, I had learned by experience my unfitness for it; and that, though the indulgence felt by George IV. towards me led him to think me the best of servants, and to ask those who displeased him how they could be so un-devonshirelike, those qualities might be less apparent to the bluff and unkinglike William.

Experience had also taught me no longer to mistake affection for loyalty.

On one of the chairs reposes a souvenir of Queen Victoria's, a cushion on which I carried one of the swords of State. To conclude the confidences into which these chairs have led me, let me farther illustrate my feelings on the subject by declaring to you, that die, as I certainly would for Queen Victoria, so would I also rather do, than become her Chamberlain.

The stamped leather, put up by the Bachelor Duke, has weathered the unfashionable years and is admired by me as it was by him. Granny disliked it intensely and tried to mask it a little by colouring here and there, which has the effect of making it more noticeable than it was before she experimented on it. She gave it up and hung green and gold cotton curtains over the lot.

The leather effigies of the Bachelor Duke round the cornice show an admirable confidence, his charming face being repeated eight times on this level. The malachite table, clock and urns were given to him by the Empress of Russia, and the Coronation chairs of George III and Queen Charlotte were perks of the Fourth Duke as Lord Chamberlain.

One of the best remembered things in the whole of Chatsworth is the door in the north wall with the *trompe l'œil* painting of a violin. Now they say it is by Vandervaart, and the door was brought from Devonshire House. Years of assiduous dusting has removed the pen and most of the rest of the carving above it, but it is the violin which takes the eye and the imagination, and after a long look at it you leave the room still undecided as to what is painted and what is real.

The State Bedroom°

The stamped leather is exactly the same in this room as in the last, but a different arrangement of the colours and gilding makes a surprising change, and this has the best effect of the two.

There are many things at Chatsworth that I should not have allowed myself to do, had I not reposed in the thoughts of being succeeded by a person so indulgent, so much attached to me as Blanche. I remember mentioning the heads upon the frieze here to her mother as an instance of one—and much on a greater scale would never have been attempted without that encouraging idea. At Leghorn, in 1839, I got the fine old cabinet of ebony and Brazil wood. This used to be the State bed-room: the furniture of it, half worn out, was sent to Hardwick. The china vases are recollections of Wingerworth, bought at a sale. Mr. Arkwright gave me the fine figured punch-bowl.

The Cloth of State comes from the Presence Chamber at Hardwick. It had been in great decay, and, after restoration, appeared too gorgeous for its old place. The arms of the second Earl, and of Christian, his wife, daughter of Lord Bruce of Kinlosse, figure in the old embroidery, upsetting the tradition of the work having been Mary Stuart's. The second Earl was born in 1590, and died in 1628.

The ceiling of this room and that of the State Dressing-Room were restored by the Gibbons brothers in the early 1970s. They gave new life to the paint, as they did in the Painted Hall, where the window recesses off the gallery were in a very bad state.

They made a sort of gipsy encampment wherever they were working, with kettles and sandwiches, to the horror of the housekeeper, and they worked long hours till the job was finished.

The Cloth of State has returned to Hardwick. Granny found the bedside tables in a stable-boy's room. She says the fireback is a fake put in by Romaine-Walker (1912). The ugly Dutch cupboard lacks a base. Granny was told by an 'expert' that such cupboards often had stone ball feet, and that is why they sometimes arrived in England without any. Rather odd reasoning?

My parents-in-law slept here during the Christmas holidays of the twenties and thirties, and icy cold it must have been.

The State Dressing-Room°

The windows here command the best view of the two gardens. Here, on the North side, stood the disproportioned door, now in the second room. There is nothing to remark here but the miniatures, two mosaics by Barberi, and the pointlace cravat, said to have been Gibbon's present at parting.

The views from here are unparalleled in the house, because it is the only room which looks south and west. For this reason my brother-in-law, Billy Hartington, chose it for his bedroom during the short time he lived here.

Granny's note says, 'Till we began to use these rooms this was a passage. A large portion of the north wall opened to give access to the crowds of tourists. We closed this partition and made a smaller door in the wall.' When she came here (1908) the lobby was a china closet with grills. She took them away and made a false wall on the west side which contains a lavatory 'a necessary convenience' she calls it. A bathroom was enclosed in part of the outer lobby.

The fireplace in the corner was put in by Granny in 1912 from the design of one at Hampton Court. The surround of local limestone she brought from a stable bedroom. She writes, 'The silver chandelier spent all its time in the plate room at Hardwick till we had it lacquered and hung here. We did not see how to hang it from any of the other painted ceilings. As it is, a cloud is an insubstantial thing from which to hang a very heavy object, but it does not do to be hypercritical.'

We decorated the walls with Oriental plates. Madame Langhan's tomb is back on the window seat. The Bachelor Duke says how handsome the old small squares of plate glass are, removed from the South Front and elsewhere, with bevelled edges, some of them almost purple. Too true, and they still make a magic effect, but it makes me wonder what was in the rest of the West Front windows before this change, and if he ever regretted the huge plate-glass panes he replaced them with on the South Front.

I wonder too what he would have thought of the brown tinted glass beloved by architects of office blocks, and even degrading the horrible new Danish Embassy in poor old Sloane Street. This year (1981) I notice that it has spread to buses, so the occupants cannot see what they have paid to go on the bus to see—the glory of the English countryside—except through what appears to be a thin film of liquid manure. What a curious idea!

The Red Room, West●

There was an opening to the State Rooms, which has been closed, and a separate communication made to the dressing-room. My childhood was greatly diverted here by the terrors of Rosalie, a maid of the beautiful Duchesse de Guiche: she was sure there were ghosts in the State Rooms. The Duchess was here in 1802, with her two brothers, Armand and Jules de Polignac. The last was a good-natured, but remarkably stupid youth, yet not without pretensions, for he wrote many verses in the albums of the day, that show him to have been as bad a poet young, as politician old.

Andrew's bedroom in 1938 to 1939. It was here he heard of the declaration of war on 3 September.

The paper was specially made by Cole's of Mortimer Street to go with the bedhead. We don't use this room now, as it is a day's march from the nearest bathroom.

The best view of the architectural plan of Chiswick House planted with box in the West Garden is from these high west windows.

It was designed to be seen from above, as that is how I got the idea for it when poring over some Kent–Burlington designs for the villa in a showcase, and it seemed to fit the place.

Part of the architectural plan of Chiswick House in golden box, west garden

The visitor, having bypassed the Red Room, goes down the West Stairs to the ground floor, but we shall go back along the Sketch Galleries, hurry through the Scots and Leicesters, and take in the rest of the second floor.

The Sketch Galleries•

You find arranged here the collection of drawings made entirely by the second Duke of Devonshire. I have classed them according to the several schools of painting; but I am sure that the arrangement must be very imperfect, and it is beyond me to make any description of the merits of this rich and valuable possession. Few things at Chatsworth are more admired. If I can obtain a good account of them, written to my mind, you shall have it — but I know not to whom to apply; amateurs would run into fanciful theories, artists would be prolix.

They hardly ever saw the light in my Father's time, nor in mine often, till I rescued them from portfolios, and placed them framed in the South Gallery below.

Before that, a very few amateurs now and then got a peep at them in London—Lawrence, Mr. Ottley, Mr. Payne Knight, and so on. Sir Thomas, mad about his own collection of drawings, got from me three studies by Raffaelle for the Transfiguration: there were five of them, and I retained the two best. I resisted long: but he was so very anxious, and so full of promises of devoted service, of painting anything for me, that I gave them at last. The way would have been to have given them for his life: he soon after died, and the sketches were sold with his collection.

The two round tables of specimens of marble were got up for me at Rome by poor Gabrielli: the other was made at Ashford. All are too like tailors' pattern books, but they are satisfactory to refer to. A vellum-bound catalogue gives the names of all in the Roman tables. I rather like that cumbrous case, made of panes of glass from the windows that used to admit darkness into the old ball-room, now library; and here I may observe, that the West front has been completely glazed with the old squares of plate glass from the South front, and elsewhere; and how handsome they are, with the bevilled edges, and some of them almost purple. They are much larger, too, those those of the East front were, of which this mineral case was made.

The old master drawings 'rescued' from their folios, have found their way back to them for the sake of their preservation.

Here are all the family portraits, the usual dingy country house parade of 'after Kneller' and 'school of Lely', from the First Earl to the present time. Hayter, Watts, Millais and de Laszlo painted the Sixth, Seventh, Eighth and Ninth Dukes (no oil painting, he). Sargent was responsible for Granny, and John Shannon painted the portrait of my mother-in-law, which I greatly love. The Oswald Birley of my father-in-law reminds me exactly of him. Billy Hartington's portrait, also by Birley, was done from photographs very soon after he was killed in 1944, and the likeness is perfect. Alas, there is no portrait of his wife, Kathleen, so I wrote to her sister, Eunice Shriver, for a photograph, and here she is in American Red Cross uniform auctioning a chicken in Bakewell Market in 1944, just before or just after her wedding. She was not beautiful, but her vitality and charm were such that she was the one who drew attention in a crowd. Her high spirits, funny American turn of phrase

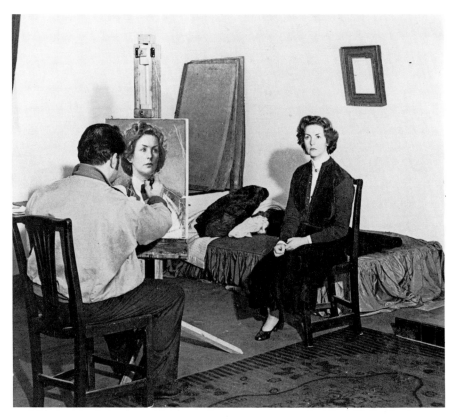

Annigoni painting me, London, 1954

and extreme good nature made her far more attractive than most pale English beauties. She was loved by everyone who knew her.

The portrait of Andrew in his robes of Chancellor of the University of Manchester by Theo Ramos is very like him. I was painted by Annigoni in 1954. He demanded many sittings, and I went to his studio in Edwardes Square every day for a month. He had done some striking portraits of dark beauties like Mary Anna Marten and Mona de Ferranti, and I realised that my colour was not his favourite. I said, 'I'm sorry about my face. I know it's not the kind you like.' He made an Italian gesture of resignation and said, 'Oh, well, it doesn't matter. It's not your fault.'

The Sketch Galleries have got some respectable furniture and tapestries, but their glory is the blue and white Delft china of the First Duke, tulip vases in profusion along the floors and shelves.

The violin: Vandervaart's *trompe l'oeil* in the State Music-Room

Diana shooting a stag: cornice of the State Bedroom

The Sabine Bedroom

The Sabine Bedroom•

The painting of the Rape of the Sabines, covering the walls in the manner of fresco painting, and said to be by Sir James Thornhill, is very handsome.

There is now a grand bed, made by Lesage of Paris, in the recess that used to be a window looking into the court.

The chimney-piece is made of a pretty, breccia-like plum-pudding stone. Altogether, this was a fine decoration quite thrown away.

A useful bedroom except for nervous guests. I am keenly criticised by Jim Lees-Milne for hanging a chandelier here. No doubt he is right, he is a purist and knows what he is on about, but the glass and candles seem to cheer up the rapists and raped. They can easily be taken away, and Jim satisfied.

Since the bed fits exactly into the recess, the bedside lamps must hook on to the wall outside, and if the lodger insists on reading he has to pick up the lamp off the hook and take it to bed with him.

Cyclamen painted on the wall by Lucian Freud, 1959

The Sabine Bathroom•

This tiny space, once a passage, just contains a bath for dwarfs and other necessities.

But it is elevated above all the other bathrooms by the portraits of outsize cyclamen painted on the wall by Lucian Freud when he stayed here in the autumn of 1959. The idea was to cover the walls with them, but Lucian is not exactly a lightning artist, and he had to leave after three flowers, three buds and a few leaves were done.

The Sabine Dressing-Room•

The dressing-room is made dingy, not to contrast too much with Sabine's gloom.

Still nice and gloomy as the Bachelor Duke so wisely recommended, because of its proximity to its dark neighbour. The extravagantly carved Victorian bed and wardrobe are very nearly back in fashion. The curtains and bed hangings and wallpaper are of such sturdy quality that they will remain in perfect condition for many more years than most of the others in the house, added to which the room is seldom used.

Granny wrote in 1940, 'The hideous hangings will never wear out. They must be about 90 years old and are as good as new.'

The Chintz Bedroom•

The Chintz room is convenient, respectable, respected.

All change here. The vast bed with green silk hangings, the curtains, bird's-eye maple pelmet board, sofa, chairs and stools, were removed from the Wellington bedroom.

The flowery wallpaper was pretty but hopelessly dirty, so I covered the walls with chintz lining called 'filling' and left the old paper under the glass guard of the electric light switches. The pelmet board over the window was too short, so its mate from the second window of the Wellington bedroom was used to enlarge it. I defy anyone to notice the seams, done by Mr Elliot, one of the best joiners in the trade.

The Chintz Dressing-Room•

The same green and silver silk curtains, bed hangings and chair covers, maple furniture and pretty domed single bed. The walls are lined with pink chintz 'filling' finished with a plain gilt fillet.

Granny dyed the carpet a virulent purple—what was she thinking of?

John Talman's (son of William) Grand Tour of Italian sightseeing is recorded in a series of drawings by Gaspar van Wittel (1653–1736).

146

The View Room[•]

The View Room—much the most popular in the house. Its views of everything, and everybody, coming, going, dwelling, must be the cause, for the furniture is bad, and the paper tawdry. Like the other end, this brings the recollection of a foreign inhabitant: here pinched the harp, and instructed in music, Mademoiselle Chersi, now Countess Macnamara. The later inhabitants fleet like a magic lantern through the thoughts, but it must be those of my mind alone.

The coldest and prettiest room on this floor. The cotton on the walls is a Boussac one which I happened on in Liberty's and thought that the big bold scale would suit the height of this room. The bed was covered in blues and mauves out of the wall cotton by George Spencer of Sloane Street.

Sophy had the View Room till she was married in 1979. During the years of her passion for horse shows the door was covered in rosettes won by this, that and the other of her beloved ponies. The bathroom has a Pugin wallpaper from the House of Lords, not at all suitable for this house but very pretty in itself.

The Plough Room[•]

The Plough Room—so named on a certain Plough Monday, a day of procession in Derbyshire, of pleasure, and of sport. In it formerly was lodged Mrs. Bunting and her dog Toujours; the most prim, and regular, and punctual of ladies' maids, walking as if she went upon wheels, generally in a riding-habit, passionately fond of horsemanship, and a hard rider. It was supposed by some that she was not averse to manship either; but that, I am persuaded, was a mistake, arising from her zeal in teaching the groom his catechism. One day, she was brought in after a tremendous fall, with her features scarcely to be distinguished, and gashes across her face and throat; and I am sure you must remember her exclamation, when she was again able to speak, addressed to you, an unwilling equestrian—"Oh, ma'am, what an encouragement this must be to your Ladyship!"

The most used of the single rooms, it has the most comfortable bed in the house and French prints all over the walls.

The Pink, Tabbaret, White Satin, Upper Bow Rooms and Armoury•

The Pink Bed-room, not pleasant, though one of the few that look to the South. It was composed of irregular odds and ends of passages, bits new and old. It smokes, moreover.

Tabberet. Not bad as a single room: in it is my Father's old bed.

White Satin. A good apartment, but cold in winter. The bed much altered, but in which no less a woman than your sister, Lady Carlisle, was born.

The Upper Bow. All these rooms fill the space that was occupied by the Nursery in former days. None are half so charming as that smoky old place, our sitting-room, looking over the Court, and seeing nothing but the smoky backs of those busts, that now decorate the roof of the old green-house.

The Armoury—another piecemeal affair—is named from a room on part of its site that contained muskets and broadswords, buff jerkins and penny trumpets, that have now disappeared from the face of day.

Some divided, one a linen-cupboard, one renamed after our cook (the Canning, not to be confused with the Prime Minister, which no doubt it soon will be) and one after a housemaid, Mrs Bater, of long standing.

The West Staircase°

The West staircase is handsome: the painted ceilings and the beautiful railing ought to produce more effect than they do. Two pictures, that were in the late Duke's bed-room and dressing-room, have an excellent light over doorways here. A Monsieur Tijou was employed for iron work in 1687: his work on this staircase was charged £40, and some iron gates and palisade £200. These are, I suppose, the gates of the West Front, now removed to the lodges. Altogether, Monsieur Tijou had £350 here, and he probably made the railings of the great stairs, and of the steps in the South front.

Harold Macmillan inspecting himself by Angela Conner

We are now on the public route again. People who come to see the house walk down these stairs from the second floor without a pause. Their steep journey is made interesting by the bronze heads of Roy Strong, John Betjeman, Paddy Leigh-Fermor, Lucian Freud, Harold Macmillan, Arnold Goodman, Andrew, and her own self-portrait by Angela Conner. Roy Strong was the first portrait in bronze that she made, and that she has gone from strength to strength is evident when you see these heads which Andrew commissioned or bought. They are worthy additions to the Bachelor Duke's beloved sculptures.

The West Sub-Corridor°

I must spare you, and will try to get on a little faster; but my task is set, and I must not shrink from it, and it must be done in my own way—telling all, or I could tell nothing.

149

This passage, being quite new, gives no recollections; but, fancy how very shallow the West front must have been without it. The door into the court stood where the opening to the West Sub-Hall now is; but it was at the foot of some steps, and those steps were out of doors, in the court, ascending awkwardly in a sort of semicircle.

The Apollino came from Wanstead; the bas-relief from Christies, this year. The great ancient Greek foot was sold to me by Carlo Finelli, the sculptor at Rome: it belonged to the Quirigi family at Lucca, and was long in their palace. The two tablets in the wall are very curious specimens of the earliest Egyptian sculpture.

The black ram's head inserted in the wall is made of basalt.

All these red portières have been got up from the drugget on which Queen Victoria walked in 1843, and many curtains besides, which must afford a proof of how good a manager your brother is. We descend now by the North Corridor and entrance-hall to the Anteroom.

The Derbyshire spar in the window is made of beautiful specimens: it shows how fine a thing might be made of the material. The stones were intended for a cabinet of minerals, and from their shape could only be arranged in a formal and not graceful pattern; and much did Sir Jeffry condemn the whole affair, which he pronounced to be the exact resemblance of his grandmother's counterpane.

This passage reminds me of coming home after a time away because the smell of the house announces more than anything else that I am back at Chatsworth. It smells of damp, clean stone and the indefinable vague tinge of polish and hyacinths in the winter, polish and people and roses in the summer.

The Derbyshire spar (bluejohn) window, condemned by Sir Jeffry Wyatville, was moved here from the theatre stairs by Andrew and the same red portières are still hanging to give the necessary splash of red along the stone corridor.

Before we head for the Chapel, there are a few rooms which are not open, but must be seen.

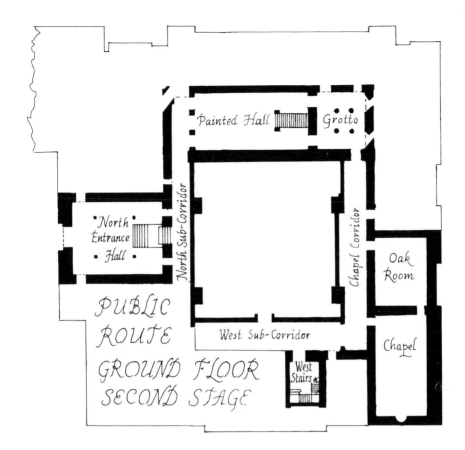

The plan shows:
- Painted Hall, Grotto (top)
- North Entrance Hall, North Sub-Corridor
- Chapel Corridor, Oak Room
- West Sub-Corridor
- West Stairs
- Chapel

PUBLIC ROUTE
GROUND FLOOR
SECOND STAGE

The Ante-Room •

This used to be the footmen's room. It had no communication with any other. It is now only a passage room, but a very convenient one.

The pictures are . . . . But here I must disclaim all intention of describing my pictures regularly to you, or of mentioning them all.

This was the telephone room when the only telephone was in a sort of shrine. In spite of the size of the house it was not unknown to lodge a male guest here when there was a big party. In the Eighth Duke's time a friend of the Duke of Portland's slept here on a camp bed and was much amused when early in the morning the letter bags were thrown on top of him, and the postman shouted, 'Get up you lazy devil, you've overslept again!'

Now it is the First Aid Room for fainting visitors.

The Bachelor Duke's Little Dining-Room●

In our youth this was the tea-room; and I declare that it had only one door, and that was under the wooden staircase at its back, now replaced by the stone one. Can you remember those wooden stairs? I can, and the feel of their painted, flat, handrail; and how the staircase was on fire; and how the confectioner, Monsieur Caille, aggravated the evil when he saw fire through the chinks of the floor under his feet, by pouring into them the contents of the kettle he was carrying, which undoubtedly fed the flame, being melted sugar: and there reigned Mary Austwick, the swarthy, venerable, and cross housemaid, peace be to her soul!

The Innkeeper at Messina required some persuasion to make him part with those horns. Altogether, this room was a failure; it is always too hot, or too cold, with an incorrigible draught. One merit it has, that of commanding the best view there is of my much-loved weeping ash, brought from Derby in 1830.

This is now a passage, and behind a screen wall which does not reach the ceiling is the gentlemen's lavatory. The walls are covered in photographs of Park Top and other racehorses of the fifties, sixties and seventies.

No wonder 'this room was a failure'. One window facing north on the ground floor is not likely to make a pleasant place in which to sit, eat or do anything else. The weeping ash survives, and its hollow trunk holds bees. Our Nanny used to blame it for the lateness of its leaves and said it was just a bunch of sticks till June. Under it Andrew has planted bulbs of every kind, and there are flowers from January till May.

Granny's Little Dining-Room (The Billiard-Room)●

When I think about this room, so many recollections crowd upon me, that I know not how to begin.

In all the days of my parents' residence here, this room, and the adjoining library, then called the Breakfast-room, were the only habitable ones they had of a morning, save when, on public days, or the occasion of some unusual visitors, they resorted to the apartment on the first floor to the South. Here, with the door opening to the cold windy passage, they sat. A plain square green baize-covered table (now in my dressing-room at Hardwick) stood between the fire and the window, then the only window to the West. Here Charles Fox, Sheridan, Hare, Lord John Townshend, Fish Crawford, and many other celebrities conversed; and there was a constant war with Hare, who did not spare the ladies of the party.

Him I can remember well, tall, the thinnest man I ever saw, his face like a surprised cockatoo, and as white. Sheridan said that, on horseback, Hare was like the shadow of Marcus Aurelius. I knew and loved Lord John Townshend, but illness, almost incessant, must have greatly changed him. The others scarcely can I recollect, only the heated features of Sheridan, and the ghastly ones of the Fish: Mr. Selwyn said of him, that he was Gonzales, a follower of the King, but secretly in love with Reynardo. Mr. Crawford, to please Dr. Johnson, who was an admirer of Dr. Donne's poetry, told him he liked Donne's poetry better than Pope's; but Dr. Johnson replied, "Sir, I can't help that."

In 1806 and the following year, I came here and began to receive and give dinners in these rooms at sixteen—a merry life. Lord Lyndoch, who has just left this world, and Lady Asgill, with a beautiful Miss Heatley, made the parties go very gaily; and many college friends used to come and stay with me—in my life's golden time.

The bookcases in this room were of the same size and construction as those in the lower library, but projecting in the manner of two opposite the windows in that room, and more prominently. My Mother was exceedingly fond of arranging the books, and it is not long since there were cards fastened to the sides of each case, with little catalogues in her handwriting; and she was always climbing up the steps, of which I have had several copies made for other parts of the house.

In later times, when Canova's statue of Madame Mère arrived, she was placed in this room, and we used to come down and look at her by lamplight.

The walls here were rather a failure: it was intended to cover them with white scagliola, but it was bad, and lustreless; and then we took to paint and varnish, rubbed down like a coach-panel. This did not look ill, but it has turned yellow, with small crevices, and is indeed like an old coach.

As a dining room this was tried for some time, and found an improvement upon the other; but it was too narrow. In vain I built a table of spare dimensions; it would not do, and it was reckoned like dining in a boat. Now the Stag parlour answers all the purposes I required here; and the green dining-room—so called from the colour of its velvet curtains—has undergone another, and I hope a last transformation.

The Billiard-table, made by Thurston, full size—which means that there is a still fuller size—is suited to the smallness of the room, and still in some positions short cues are necessary. The table, of bird's-eye maple, is a chef d'œuvre of workmanship, and has been pronounced excellent by no less a man than "Jonathan."

Nearly every room in the house has been a billiard room at some time. When Victor and Evie lived here this was the small dining-room where the family ate when they were alone. It was 102 yards from the kitchen. Now it is used by people who come to look at papers. It is cold and narrow and high, and does not invite a long stay.

It is strange that the Bachelor Duke's father and Georgiana and their guests should have used this room and its neighbour so much, as they can never have had the charm and lightness of the first floor rooms which face south.

My mother-in-law put the cupboards from Devonshire House against the walls, and in them are letters and diaries, photograph books, game books and visitors' books galore. Here we meet if there are plans to discuss, or papers to be spread out on the only table in the house which is not already covered in things. I remember Mr Pearce, architect of the 1970 greenhouse, going from room to room vainly looking for somewhere to show us his plans and muttering, 'These stately homes are all very well but there is *nowhere* to put *anything.*'

The Duke's Sitting-Room (The Lower Library) •

The pilasters were there, the marble chimneypiece was there, and they must find it difficult to recognize each other. No other trace remains of the old breakfast-room. It had a lower and plain whitewashed ceiling : the entire room was white, except the marble wainscot at the end, then dingy and unpolished. The bas-reliefs, now in the gallery, formed the decoration— Moses over the chimney, in a fine wooden frame of strawberry leaves ; and children squeezing grapes, between the windows. There were deep wooden window-seats, rather pleasant, and the recesses had small bookcases contrived in them. Two large leather chairs, with outspreading arms, guarded the sides of the fire.

From this description it might be supposed that this was not so bad a room and decoration ; but my sister must know better,—and you, posterity, take my word for it, it was atrocious.

Mr. John Crace, the upholsterer, was the magician who transformed it into its present state, making it look something between an illuminated MS., and a café in the Rue de Richelieu. I had wished to have one room in the new style of decoration, and in a short time two or three bearded artists in blouses were imported from Paris, and completed the ceiling and pilasters. The names of the most skilful were Holfeld for the figures, and for the ornaments, &c. (they willingly copied from nature the flowers I brought them) Messrs. Govaerts, Haclin, Van Hoot, and Glover. The heads of authors in the medallions were selected and placed there without my knowledge—so marches intellect with art ; but Mr. John Crace said that I must supply inscriptions: accordingly, Mrs. Lamb gave that for Shakespeare, Lord Morpeth for Pope, and the rest were chosen by my intelligent friend and librarian, Mr. J. Payne Collier.

Homer, Anacreon, Horace, Virgil, Cicero, and Livy have no scrolls.

This room, small as it is, contains more than five thousand seven hundred volumes: the lowest shelves hold the largest books, and they are not the largest size of octavo. I purchased the library of Dampier, Bishop of Ely, and many of its treasures are here. The arrangement is copied from that of Lord Spencer's library, both here and upstairs.

I cannot go away without notice of the doors, on which the counterfeit volumes are certainly not the least admired works in my library ; and for fear you should not have studied them sufficiently, I shall make an extract from the catalogue that has been exclusively compiled for them. The chief contributor to this literary undertaking was Mr. Thomas Hood ; but some friends here, when the doors were in progress, threw in their assistance ; among others. Mrs. Arkwright, and Lady Teresa Lewis. Is it surprising that the door attracts?

Barrow on the Common weal.
Blower on the Trade winds.
Boyle on Steam.
Brunel's Hole Duty of Man.
Burnet's Theory of the Conflagration.
Cherry on the Currency.
Cleopatra's Pearl, by the venerable Bede.
[etc]

    I do not know why there was an omission of one in the alphabetical order, good from its intentional badness,

    Count Erfeit Wolswear, or Memoirs of Theodore Weconsele,

invented by the wife of a dear and never forgotten friend, who loved and almost belonged to Chatsworth.

    The Library is warmed by Price's Apparatus, which is fixed partly in the cellar under the Leather Room, and partly under the West Corridor. The heat is regulated by valves at the top and bottom of a bookcase on the East side of the room. The ventilation is carried on by an air-drain from an area in the West front. The same Apparatus also warms the West Sub-Hall, the Chapel, and the Western end of the North Corridor.

An interviewer asked Andrew why he referred to his room as his sitting-room rather than his study. 'Because I sit in it more than I study', was the answer.

    The decoration of the bearded Frenchmen from Paris remains unchanged, thank goodness, and must surely have been by the same hands as that of the Grand Véfour restaurant in the Palais Royal.

    This and the Leather Room next door are housemaid's nightmares, so varied and so spread are the piles of books, newspapers, magazines and yearbooks on the floor and window seats, so covered are the tables in letters and oddments, as well as pictures piled against one another leaning against the bookshelves. It is no wonder that a French friend of mine coming here for the first time threw up his hands when he saw this remarkable mess and exclaimed over what he called the *désordre britannique*.

The Leather Room—*désordre britannique*

157

The Leather Room•

The Leather Room has been enlarged by taking a passage, of the width of that still remaining behind the Lower Library; it was paved with stone. The walls were plain deal wainscot, and the picture of Flying Childers was opposite the fire: it is now hung with cuir repoussé from Bernheim et Cie, at Paris. It was to have been the Auditor's Room, and the medallions on the ceiling do represent all the attributes and virtues that such an officer should have; but Mr. B. Currey found it too fine, and, the leather being excellent for the sound of music, I have placed the piano-forte here, under the nose of poor Bellini, whose bust, by Dantan Jeune, fills an angle of the room.

An extension of Andrew's room and more or less a passage now, lined with bookcases stuffed with the ubiquitous books and even more paintings leaning against them.

The West Entrance-Hall•

Large folding-doors into the court had over them two small panes of bad glass, that made the darkness of this room visible. The other door only admitted light when open, which the wind usually took care that it should be; and it was a damp, mouldy place. Still, I must allow that, when all the doors were open, the view from the West into the court, with Arion and his cistern in the middle, was very handsome and palatial. Great comfort is gained, and Sir J. Wyatville was very desirous of removing all appearance of the entrance to the house being in the West front. There are prints of it, with coaches and six driving to the foot of the steps under the West terrace.

The ornamented cove is old, and I think it beautiful. The ceiling was painted in chiaro oscuro—without merit and much damaged; and a restorer of pictures having made it, to my mind, infinitely worse, I had it painted over with distemper, which can easily be removed: therefore, if anybody should ever want to see a sprawling figure of Fame, blowing a trumpet with all her might, and holding a design of the West front, "Cujus Fama volat," accompanied by two Cupids in wigs, they have only to wash.

Ceiling of West Entrance Hall

West Entrance Hall: Canova's head of
Napoleon (note weighing-machine on right)

*The floor is made of Neapolitan tiles, a copy of the recently found mosaic
of Alexander and Darius, at Pompeia; and the "Cave Canem" was also
there in a porch, and Mr. Paxton gave me this copy of it.*

Sir Jeffry Wyatville would be surprised to find that we are back where
he started, and once again it is our front door. Instead of coaches and six,
dull cars and winter Land-Rovers use the drive, which was a garden path
till 1959.

The ceiling was washed before my time and the bewigged cupids and
sprawling Fame are visible again. Mr Thompson said the ceiling and the
stone frieze carved by Nadauld are part of the original decoration. He
wondered if the extremely bad ceiling painting could be a first attempt at
working from a cradle by Thornhill.

The weighing machine is a relic of the passion for weighing visitors
which ruled in the early 1900s. Visitors' books here and at Lismore
record the weights, as well as the names, of all who came.

The two big horse paintings, Flying Childers, always described as by

159

Wootton, but now said to be by James Seymour, and Scarr by Wootton came from the Eighth Duke's house at Newmarket after his death in 1908.

A framed and faded note beside Flying Childers says 'September 28th 1719. This is to certify that the bay stoned horse His Grace the Duke of Devonshire bought of me was bred by me and was 5 years old last grass and no more. Leo Childers.'

The Mineral Room•

These cases were my Mother's; they were upstairs near her dressing-room. The right hand case contains her collection of Derbyshire minerals. In the other of foreign ones, there are some specimens I added, and some that Dr. Creighton assisted me in procuring at St. Petersburg, where I gave some Derbyshire and Cornwall ores in exchange.

The most remarkable thing here is a large crystal of emerald: it was brought by Don Pedro from Brazil. All these minerals are in a disgraceful state of neglect and want of classification. Those collected by my Mother ought to be replaced in their former order, as they were in the days of White Watson of Bakewell, who in vain endeavoured to hammer mineralogy into our youthful heads.

All the bits of marble I ever picked up abroad form a pavement in the window recess here; and it is the best way of disposing of such relics. I have had the maladresse to forget which bit came out of Santa Sophia at Constantinople: it was a very small one. This work may be much more neatly done, vide a table in the statue gallery, but the expense is much greater: thus roughly joined, it does very well for flooring.

This space can hardly be called a room; it is just a passage with a window. The cases of Georgiana's minerals were here when I first knew the house, and had to be passed when calling on Mr Thompson in his lair. It was on one of these visits that Mr Thompson showed my sister Nancy the 'diseased' stones which had destroyed the paper they rested on and were beginning to eat into the wooden shelf. She was so struck by the idea of ill stones that she described them in one of her books.

Now it is occupied by broken fishing-rods, macintoshes and boots left

The Duke's Sitting-Room

The Chapel, with the names on the backs of the chairs of the ladies who
embroidered their seats

Francis Thompson, librarian

behind by shooting guests (always for giants or dwarves, never a decent 36, and so no good to me). There are tennis shoes with no laces, rusty gardening tools of immense weight, an incomplete croquet set and dog dishes and biscuits—altogether an area best avoided by the tidy or the squeamish.

The Flower Room (Lord Frederick's Room)•

Lord Frederick had not a very comfortable room, with doors on all sides, and steps up and down; and the mineral room was the coldest of lodgings. Why Lord Frederick's name alone has descended with his room I know not: I can remember him, a great uncle, living at Twickenham, where Lord Ailsa's place, St. Margaret's, now is. He died in 1803. He left £100 to each of his great nephews and nieces, and £500 to such as were his god-children.

Look at that old triangular oak cabinet, bought of Mr. Hull when he left Youlgreave; and the bust by Bartolini of Countess Marie Potocka; and the small slabs of rare ancient marbles: also the carpets made of cats'-skins. Are there not curiosities in this room?

A door was opened by me into a private seat in the Chapel—most convenient: the curious lock upon it was found at Devonshire House, rescued perhaps from the great fire that destroyed so much there in 1733.

This room will always remind me of Mr Thompson, the very archetypal librarian, already old when I first knew him, white face and hands, a tonsure of yellow-white hair showing under a black skull-cap. He was one of those lucky people whose face is arranged in a smile even in repose. He lived in Edensor and journeyed across the park in an incredible machine known as the Flying Saucer. It was an electric three-wheeler which looked for all the world like a bath-chair from the sea-front at Brighton. It bore him noiselessly along the drive at its one pace to his big desk and his work in this friendly, sunny, west-facing room. He was wonderfully uncritical of our philistine lack of interest in the marvellous things in his care. How often now I wish I had asked him a thousand questions and listened carefully to the answers.

He was helped by Tom Wragg, son of the master of Edensor village school. Their partnership began in 1934 and lasted till Mr Thompson's death in 1964, when Tom succeeded him in the job and was himself librarian till he died in 1978.

The door to the Chapel has been blocked up. A large sink was put under the window in 1959, and it has become the flower room. Guns are cleaned, and unhouse-trained dogs lodge here. Philip Jebb has designed bookcases. The Brazilian Swetenia wood for the shelves lies in the carpenter's shop, and John Oliver is poised to make yet another library to hold the books now on the floor in the attic.

We go into the Chapel by way of the West Corridor and Chapel Corridor.

The Chapel Corridor°

Here you have no grand pavement, as opposite, but you have a lighter, broader passage. It used certainly to be the most dreary bit of the house, a bleak open colonnade. The Chapel door opened widely into it, and two dark passages were cut off from the present tea-room and the Oak-room, to let people up a flight of four broken steps into the garden. The carved stone of the chimneypieces came from the Sub-Hall. I bought the two old coffers at Rome, and the wooden figure of Time: it supported a frame for a clock, and it would look well as a stand for the reading-desk or pulpit in the Chapel.

I put the brass lamps, hideously electrified, along this passage.

The caique seems to have found a permanent berth here. Next to it used to be marble head of Lord Byron, and the association of Byron with the Bosphorus was taken a step further by Granny, who inadvertently started a legend that it was Byron's boat.

The Chapel°

The Chapel is the least altered place at Chatsworth: painted by Verrio, carved by Gibbons, what could be left for Sir Jeffry to do? The sole change is, that the pavement, which had sunk, owing to a settlement of the walls, has been made level with much difficulty; and the warm air introduced is not only useful here, but keeps the drawing-rooms above free from damp on opening the gallery-door.

There is all I have to say about the Chapel—except, that to-day I remarked the beauty of its key, which, having an Earl's coronet, shows that the whole must have been finished before the creation of the first Duke in 1694.

The Bachelor Duke dismisses this glorious place in a few sentences, not for lack of appreciation, but because he wisely left well alone. The chairs placed in rows facing each other are the ones whose seats and backs were worked in *gros point* by his friends with their names painted on them.

Daily prayers were said till 1914 and a service was held on Sundays till 1939. The chief thing remembered by the participants was that the men sat on one side with the women opposite, and the peculiar agony of church giggles happened to them all every Sunday. The youngest children and their nannies sat in the gallery. They sometimes managed to push a prayer book over the ledge to crash on to the floor below and make a welcome diversion.

Now we have a carol service in the chapel on the Sunday before Christmas, and it is a rare pleasure to listen to the loved old tunes and gaze at the extraordinary beauties of marble and wood and paint.

The Oak Room °

One day, walking with a friend in Berners Street, we were tempted into the auction-room, and found carved oak being knocked down. I bought to the right and left, and became possessed of almost all that you see here, the fittings of some German monastery, and the woodwork of an old-fashioned pew. So inconsiderate a purchase was never made—however, look at the result. Is it not charming? What discussions might be raised upon it hereafter!—what names given to the busts, unknown to the buyer as they were to the seller! The second individual from the door appears to have been an avaricious prelate, if we take the dog gnawing a bone to have been his emblem.

This room, supported by props and furnished with temporary shelves, first received Mr. Cavendish's library, presented to me by my uncle, Lord George Henry Cavendish, when he got the rich inheritance from that philosopher— the man who weighed the world, and buried his science and his wealth in solitude and insignificance at Clapham. It was also the dormitory of poor Dicky Smith, the Chaplain; and to this room I remember banishing the learned Parr, when he insisted on having a room to smoke in—a desire then (1813) considered most atrocious and derogatory. Of late years, when family prayers have been read, this has been the suitable place for them; and when the Grand Duke Michael Paulowitsch arrived on a visit last year at a very late hour, here he had the gayest-looking supper, which contrasted agreeably with the dingy walls, and looked like a jolly friar's repast.

Henry VIII.'s rosary, designed by Holbein, stands on the table. Since his time it has belonged to the Père de la Chaise, who had left it to the establishment of the Jesuits in Paris, and, when their goods were sold, it was bought by the Abbé Brotier, editor of Tacitus; and the nephew of Brotier sold it to Messieurs Rundell and Bridge, and they to me. It cost as much as all the woodwork in the room—£200. Was that much or little?

The red silk circumstance beneath it was worked by her Majesty Queen Adelaide. On the chimneypiece there are two curious ancient incense burners, from the collection of Dr. Butler, Bishop of Lichfield. The China vases were given to me by Mrs. Peterson. The octagon oak table is modern; the square one, placed behind the reading-desk, used to form the frail support of the pulpit in the Chapel. People here are very apt to say Baldachino. Having mentioned Mr. Smith as inhabiting this room, I must remind you of him. He

Oak Room carving

Monkey table from the Great Exhibition in the Oak Room

was the type of a Fellow of a College; he was tutor at Cambridge to William Cavendish, Lord George's eldest son; and my Father, at Lord George's request, placed him at Edensor. He was, with Charles Cavendish, thrown out of the cart when the fatal accident occurred at Holker,* and had a most narrow escape. He was a chatty and lively man, well read in the classics, too fond of punning, and willing to be everybody's butt, and especially that of his numerous pupils; thoughtless, improvident, ready always to do everything, to go everywhere, to travel, to ride, to dance, to act, to sing. He was fond of his parishioners, and those who remember him talk of him with regard. He had the misfortune to outlive his intellect and his cheerfulness, and for several years before his death it was melancholy to see him. A picture of him, like but bad, hangs in the little dining-room. On the whole, Mr. Smith may be said to have been regarded with good-will by those with whom he was acquainted, and he was an affectionate, kind father.

*William Cavendish (1783–1812), father of the Seventh Duke, was killed in this accident.

This is certainly the oddest room in the house. The oak carvings are bizarre, to say the least. Some look like mad Boy Scouts or Boer War heroes, one is my idea of Good King Wenceslas with a troop of courtiers, and they might all be portraits of my father and his brothers. I once had the fancy to paint this room blue and white. I am glad that I resisted. It is unchanged by us, except for the new entrance to the Chapel, necessary for the circulation of people in summer.

What has happened to the picture of Mr Smith? I wish I knew.

Beyond the Oak Room is the present Billiard Room, and two or three other rooms not open to the public.

The Stag Parlour•

This was poor Mrs. Gregory's bed-room. Here she lived and died. What a change! The heavy iron props (placed to sustain the weight of what was going on in the then dining-room above) are removed; the excess of cheerfulness replaces the extreme of dulness and gloom. This is now become the breakfast-room, and morning place of refuge for the idle. The chimneypiece came from the summer parlour at Chiswick, from which it had been removed, chimney and all, to make a doorway for the Emperor Nicolas to go to his breakfast.

Why this room was called the Stag Parlour, why abandoned with its sunny aspect, are mysteries unknown to me. Nothing can be more convenient, for a door opens into the new tea-room, and the entrance to the pleasure ground by the East lobby cannot fail to be the most popular way of getting out of doors.

Observe the most curious of locks on the door to the South-East sitting-room. It was on the door of the Den in the North front, and augmented my childish awe and respect for that redoubtable room. Each time the door is unlocked the dial turns round, but it must have revolved one hundred times before the cipher below advances. To bolt the door, you pull the man's hat over his eyes; to detect the key-hole, you touch the spring under his foot. What a lock!

The Smoking-Room till our time, for men, and the only place where a drink before meals could be found.

Lock in the Stag Parlour

Its present strange decoration of black and gold wallpaper above the Victorian wainscot was ordered by Sto and Emma when we moved here. They were fifteen and sixteen years old, and the Stag Parlour was their sitting-room and their club. You had to be a member of the club to be allowed in. The upper age limit was twenty-one. Uncle Harold Macmillan was staying here when Prime Minister and naturally wandered in to revive old memories. He was sharply turned out as a non-member and ineligible for membership.

Uncle Harold has suffered some rough treatment as a guest. I have never been much good at *place à table* (John Wyndham used to do it by weight, which didn't go down too well with smart foreigners) and after a long day on the moor at Bolton I am more gaga than usual and quite unable to think. After such a day, and at a time of the usual political crisis, I looked down the dinner table and saw the Prime Minister seated between two boys in their first year at Eton, Sto and Richard Beckett. The Prime Minister was obviously preoccupied with his own thoughts, and the boys were anxiously casting around for a suitable subject of conversation. After what seemed like an endless silence I heard Sto say, 'Uncle Harold, *Old Moore's Almanack* says you'll *fall* in October.' To his eternal credit, after a suitable pause for consideration, the P.M. answered, 'Yes, I should think that's about right.'

Since Sto and Em are married and gone it has again become a convenient room for breakfast when there are a lot of people as it is next to the pantry.

The Tea Room next door is our billiard-room. In the inevitable bookcases round the walls are fat volumes like *The Grouse in Health and Disease*, *With the High Peak Harriers*, and *The Gun at Home and Abroad*.

The Pantry (The South-East Sitting-Room) •

The changes by which I have gained so much here are from adding some space to what was a bath in the corner of the house. It was never used in my recollection. The marble was removed, and cut up for the new baths, and for other purposes, nobody ever contemplating the release of the room from the housekeeper's monopoly. The ceiling is beautifully painted; and bold will be the artist who undertakes to rival it in the two other compartments that remain to be filled up. For decoration here, I have placed hastily the following pictures, that do so well, I am not inclined to disturb them. Do not despise the portraits of my favourite dogs, who have been few, but in general long-lived. At the north end you see Betty Martin, a most beautiful terrier given to me by dear old Lord Essex. She is accompanied by Idol, a prodigious mongrel, who lived to a great age, and was at last demolished by a fierce mad dog, who rushed into the garden at Chiswick, and ate her up while peaceably seated by a monkey, her particular friend. Martin died of the distemper, young; the picture is by Chalon, the likeness exact: the view of Chiswick is as bad as the dogs are like. He also painted Spot, who hangs on the East side: she was an Italian greyhound, born at Florence, and died full of years. On the same side you have Tawney, a black spaniel, given to me by Lady Castlereagh, at a time when there was nothing so rare as that breed, allowed only to exist at Arundel Castle, where Jockey of Norfolk restricted their number, and nourished his owls with the superabundant population of puppies. This picture was painted at Rome by a German, named Peter, of much celebrity, established there. The Coliseum, and the Palace of the Cæsars, supposed to be Tawney's favourite resorts, are in the background. Bony and Var are by Edwin Landseer. To speak of living dogs appears superfluous, and, in this case, unnecessary, for surely their names are European. The head of Bony was the study for his introduction as a reporter in the picture at Chiswick, called the Poodle laying down the law [Trial by

Jury]. On the South side are some pointers, by Desportes, a painter employed in the service of Louis XIV., who came to England in the train of the Duc d'Aumont, ambassador. On the collar of one of the dogs is "A Mylord Burlington:" it must have been Richard, the last Earl, at that time eighteen years of age. To the West are some lapdogs, with the name Knight [Knijff], and the date 1698—belonging, I suppose, to Charles, Earl of Burlington. There are two smaller pieces, one of dogs hunting a wild boar, the other of poultry; which, with all the canine works excepting Bony, remained for many years at Ashford Rookery.

The pictures have gone and are spread round the house because this room is now the pantry. The lift to the Dining-Room leaves from a door in the corner. The painted ceiling is carefully preserved under a new, lower, one. Younger generations please note it could easily be changed back to its former glory. This is the room in which Granny's secretary Miss Saunders worked, and was a haven for the Aunts when they wanted to escape from governesses and parents.

Trial by Jury by Sir
Edwin Landseer

The East Lobby•

From unwillingness to disturb Hannah Gregory, the house-keeper who dwelt here for half a century, there had been no attempt made to alter the distribution of these the most agreeable rooms at Chatsworth. The East Lobby almost forms a part of the Grotto Room. Five slabs of Oriental granite, with rough edges, ill-suited for tables, with five others of Aberdeen granite, form a centre, like a marble carpet. The five first were almost my earliest purchase at Rome, in 1819. The Duke of Hamilton would have me buy them, and I gave twice their value, for which poor Gaspare Gabrielli, the worthy painter who executed most honestly all my subsequent commissions, never ceased to rebuke me. Here they now repose; and a sixth, divided into four parts, decorates the stone pedestal of the Medicis Vase in the Orangery.

The East Lobby keeps its granite floor, over which passes every morsel of food from the kitchen to the lift in the pantry and thence to the Dining-Room above.

   Next to it is the Grotto, on the public route.

The Grotto°

Considering the former condition of this room, it is inconceivable that so much money should have been laid out on its decoration. It had no opening to the east; it had a small door to the South Colonnade, and a dingy window to the court, and it was almost dark at midday. The same stones that form the pavement at the foot of the great staircase above are elaborately carved beneath, and form the ceiling here. The Venus fountain and the garlands over the niches are made of Roche Abbey stone; and the cistern is of black Ashford marble. For what purpose so dark a place can have served, there is no saying.

We have put lighted showcases here to enliven this dark corner. There are some presents from official visitors of Andrew's far off Commonwealth days and orders presented to my mother-in-law when she was Mistress of the Robes to the Queen from 1953 to 1966, brilliant silks in all colours of the rainbow given by Kings, Emperors and Presidents,

The Grotto

some deposed, some murdered and some, surprisingly, still going strong. When you emerge from the Grotto you find yourself back in the Painted Hall. Now we go through it again and up the Oak Stairs for the last lap.

The Oak Stairs°

This Staircase, connected with the Painted Hall above and below, was one of Sir Jeffry Wyatville's best efforts. He rather wished to add another flight of steps to the floor above, but that I resisted. There was a wooden staircase here, with no communication to the hall, very steep and dreary.

The picture of George IV. was one of a great number supplied by Sir Thomas Lawrence for the Ambassadors and other official persons. I accompanied William IV. one day to Kensington Palace, and found a room full of them, where he gave me this one.

Dawe, R. A., painted the Emperor for me at Moscow: it was the first portrait of him in the Imperial robes, and it was brilliantly lit up for the Fête I gave to him and the Empress in the Maison Batascheff, or Schépéloff, for my house had plenty of names. It was very like him then. Dawe also painted the Empress, later.

The Duke of Cumberland, by Sir Joshua Reynolds, long stood over the chimneypiece in the yellow drawing-room.

A cavern of great gloom in spite of being 'one of Sir Jeffry Wyatville's best efforts'. Perhaps the decoration carried out by Turner Lord of Mount Street in 1929 adds unfairly to this depressing quarter, but I would not like to change it, as it is typical of its time, even to the stippled paint on the plaster (which pretends to be stone) and the heavy cornice which Granny and Romaine-Walker added to break the height. Stippling was all the rage in the 1920s. I remember my mother's delight at the dining-room in our house in Rutland Gate, where the walls were just like these, and I notice it is now beginning to come back in fashion. The poor brown brocade is not my taste, but it has a horrid sort of suitability.

Certainly the communication the stairs give is much appreciated, since so many people pass this way. Granny put the jib doors to the Bachelor Passage, and very necessary they are.

I have made an addition here by rescuing the extraordinary brass and stag's horn chandelier from the garage, where it hung for years, beautifully wrapped in brown paper. Hanging it from the dome was a hazardous job (it is extremely heavy) carried out by Mr Shimwell and company as though it was a most ordinary thing to be asked to do. The

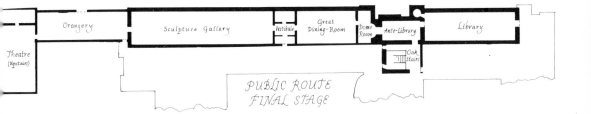

Orangery

Sculpture Gallery

Vestibule

Great Dining-Room

Dome Room

Ante-Library

Library

Theatre (Upstairs)

Oak Stairs

PUBLIC ROUTE
FINAL STAGE

huge picture of the Bachelor Duke was given to Andrew by the City of Derby when the Guildhall was altered in 1971.

The Library°*

We used to call this the Gallery. The old ceiling remains, the frieze alone is new. Upon the walls were painted panels, now inserted in the ceiling of the Ball-room. The floor was deal; there were white painted window-seats. It was difficult to light, but made a pretty ball-room. In 1815 I began to pull out the panels, and convert them into bookcases, by doing which I not only endangered the security of the walls, but approached certain flues much too nearly. For books the room is now well suited; it is only too narrow, and Sir Jeffry Wyatville's plan for a projection opposite the fireplace, taking in two windows, would have been a great improvement, but I dislike the appearance it would have had outside.

The chimneypiece is new; the palm branch ornaments were suggested by some above the doorway in the West front. The vases of Siberian Jasper were given to me by the Emperor Nicolas. The gallery, with the rail of what was called Mosaic gold, is very useful and convenient. The staircase in the corner is in the same situation as an old one that existed in the walls.

Through all the changes this room has undergone, its present shape is, to my mind, the best. We did not presume to change anything in the 1950s except to re-arrange the furniture. The shabby paint of the shutters and the panels under the windows, the dingy ceiling where it is neither

*The Library is not open to visitors, but one can peer in very satisfactorily and see it from the Ante-Library.

173

pictures nor gilt, is not annoying to me, at least not as annoying as I fear new paint would be.

Books from floor to ceiling, surrounded by mahogany and brass, are I think the best decoration of all, and with decent Devonshire House sofas and chairs and many curiosities lying around on the folio tables the library has a completely different air from any of the other rooms in the house. It looks its best at night with the curtains drawn and the fire going, brass, mahogany, leather spines and gilt titles catching the light and making an atmosphere of comfort and calm.

The curtains, made of the Bachelor Duke's cut velvet from the walls of the Blue Drawing-Room and hung here by him, survive, but are beginning to suffer from age and too much light. There is a good example in this room of the harm done by light, that most penetrating and destructive enemy of the housekeeper.

The mahogany door, which is ever open during the hours when people come round, is skewbald. Half of it is colourless and dry where the light hits it, and the other half is what a polished mahogany door is meant to look like.

When I said we did nothing here, it is not strictly true. The little winding stone staircase behind the bookcases at the south end, which took you to the gallery, was used for the new food lift from the pantry to the Dining-Room, so the way up was blocked. Luckily there was another staircase at the north end, but it by-passed this floor, so in 1964 a doorway was cut through bookcase and stone, and you can reach the gallery once more. We were told that for various technical reasons it would not be possible to do this. Messrs Fisher and Oliver (comptroller and house carpenter) are not men to be daunted by the impossible, and done it was, so skilfully that it could always have been there. It is so like this house to provide a second staircase when it was needed, and so like its guardians to do the impossible.

Now we had a door to cover with false book-backs, like its mate at the other end of the room, waiting for names. Paddy Leigh-Fermor thought of the best; *Sideways Through Derbyshire* by Crabbe, *Gloucester in All Weathers* by Doctor Foster, *Consenting Adults* by Abel N. Willing, *Jellies and Blancmanges* by Somerset, *Venus Observed* by I. Sawyer, *The Day after Gomorrah* by the Bishop of Sodor and Man, *Intuition* by Ivor Hunch, *Dipsomania* by Mustafa Swig, *The Battle of the Bulge* by Lord Slim, and *Alien Corn* by Dr Scholl. *Studies in Sentiment* by E. Motion

The Library

somehow got separated from its twin *Reduced to the Ranks* by D. Motion. Old family jokes *Also Ran* by Antrim, *The Liverpool Sound* by Viscountess Mersey and *Troubled Waters* by M. I. T. Ford complete the set. Lovely books with no insides.

The grand leather spines were made by Sangorski & Sutcliffe. I never heard whether the man who did them was amused or thought them too silly for words.

My favourite of all the books in the library is *Ronalds on the Apple*, with exact illustrations of 314 kinds of apples precisely described in the language of the specialist. Their names are evocative of kitchen gardens of yesteryear: Hoary Morning, Bedfordshire Foundling, Seek No Further, Cornish Aromatic, Large White Incomparable, Dutch Minion, Winter Strawberry, Hanwell Souring, Striped Monstrous Reinette and Hall Door. Ask people what these names refer to and you will find your friends you thought were of scholarship material are stumped.

They remind me of that immaculate kitchen gardener, Mr Chester, who ruled over eleven acres enclosed by high walls at Barbrook in the park and produced wondrous fruit and vegetables there till it was abandoned in 1946. His standards were as high as those of Lord Waterford's gardener at Curraghmore who, on being told the time of one-thirty for a luncheon party said, 'Then I will cut the asparagus at twelve.'

The Ante-Library°

A Billiard-room in old times—small, being the square part only of what you see now: very dark. From a window to the North you looked down upon a sort of dingy, semi-subterraneous street, wet and coal-coloured, enlivened here and there by heaps of ashes. It backed the old offices, and had an opening through a low arch into a sunk fence, and so to the park.

The room was surrounded with panels, some of which, with those taken from the library, are much admired in the ceiling of the ball-room: one represents a design for the West front, with some variation. When they were taken down, Sir Jeffry Wyatville asked me to give them to him for the decoration of his tower in the new buildings at Windsor: I am not sorry now

The shop in the Orangery

Henry VIII's rosary

The Emperor Fountain and the Statue of Endymion

to have declined. Altogether, I have not given away near so much in my time as was to be expected. To be sure, when Lord and Lady Dumfermline established themselves at Stubbing Court, and repaired it, I sent a whole cartload of Gibbon's carving, that was lying unemployed in the lumber-room, to decorate their drawing-room, little foreseeing that I should become so eager a collector of carved wood afterwards. When they went to live in Scotland, I thought of getting it back; but, on finding that it was highly valued and going to be removed with care, I became consoled and satisfied. Some of the festoons had the initials of the first Duke at their base. If, however, that much respected pair could have taken Chatsworth away with them, instead of a few pieces of wood, they should have been welcome to do so, for to them affection and gratitude are due from me.

Sir Jeffry managed the additions to this house most admirably. My wish expressed to him was to have a suite of rooms, especially a good dining-room, in this direction. It was not easy to adapt a new building to the corner of a square house, but it was successfully accomplished here by the kind of tribune he invented—keeping the central line, and yet not projecting offensively on the outside towards the East.

The unusual shape of the room caused no objection. I admire an irregular room, if it is composed of regular parts; and the same maxim is good for a house, and eminently so for this Chatsworth.

While beginning my alterations here, I made several journeys into Italy, and at Rome the love of marble possesses most people like a new sense, and a knowledge is acquired of the value of the ancient marbles; an expression to be applied, I take it, to such as have not their quarries known, and are known not to be natural to Italy, where, however, Roman magnificence has made their remains so plentiful, that you find streets paved, as it were, with their fragments. This taste awakened, I did not scruple, in 1819, to purchase two columns for £2000. Unluckily, or luckily, for me, Pius VII. built the Braccio Nuovo of the Sculpture Gallery in the Vatican: an embargo was laid upon the exportation of all columns, and some time after, mine, the most beautiful in the world, were taken to adorn the middle window of that new arm: they were made of Alabastro-Cotognino. Of course I had not paid, and I did not take the Prince Royal, now King of Bavaria's line, which was to maintain his purchase, and tire out the Papal patience; as in the case of the Barberini Sleeping Faun, which he allowed to remain for many years in its packing-case at Rome. After this defeat, judge of my joy at being informed in London, that there lay in the garden at Richmond House some precious columns, in cases half devoured by the dry rot (happily it does not digest marble) and that they were to be sold. I went, saw, and bought for a price, in comparison, ridiculously small, and acquired eight columns of surpassing beauty for not more than £50 each—and four of them, two being of the finest oriental alabaster (giallastro) and two of Pavonazzetto, embellish this tribune.

The two vases of Occhio di Paone, a marble so rare that there is no specimen of it in the galleries of the Vatican, found so good a place here that I did not remove them to the Sculpture Gallery, with the rest of the marbles, on its completion.

One of Hayter's first pictures is placed here in the ceiling. The excellent light for it, the colouring, and the etherial subject, must compensate for the infra. dig. of its position. Mr. Charles Landseer in the medallions gave colour to Thorwaldsen's groups of Day and Night.

The clear glasses were the first I placed here: they are the greatest ornament of modern decoration. Nothing struck me so much in Russia as the vast windows of single panes; and it is a fashion that, although followed and even exceeded by half the shops in London, must still retain its charm. The round slab, with inlaid work, was made in India for Lady William Bentinck.

The carpets are English, made at Axminster, and they wear much better and fade less than the French; but Sir Jeffry longed for them to fade: he thought the bright colours destroyed the effect of the room and ceiling.

This room is well known to you as the place of rendezvous before dinner. I find that most formal, weariest, hungriest moment of life less painful when the patients are squeezed together in a small compass; there is less space for their ceremonies, their shyness, and their awkwardness. When more than twenty-two, we congregate in the Library, and on very great occasions in the Drawing-room—from which the march is awful. Now, dinner is ready.

We reached this room in October 1963, and the dark, smoky, dirty, paint was replaced by white, and the gold was washed and came up like new.

We left the Bachelor Duke's 'clear glass', or plate glass, window here for a special reason; when you stand opposite it in the garden and look through it the looking-glass over the fireplace reflects the garden back at you and has a droll effect. Granny removed the looking-glass and its very ornate frame. I brought it from the granary store and put it back where it belongs.

In 1965 we gave a ball for Sto on his twenty-first birthday and we received the guests here, danced in the Great Dining-Room and had supper in the Sculpture Gallery. The statues were draped in ivy for the night, and it suited them down to the ground.

The Dome Room°

This is where the wing of 1827 joins the old house, and where the Bachelor Duke's passion for marble begins to show.

In the next three rooms there is marble in every shape, colour and form; pillars, vases, plinths, urns, tazzas, table-tops, heads, bodies and legs of men, women and children, mythological wings supporting mythological horses, dogs, babies and snakes in every pattern of salami, brawn, liver sausage, galantine, ballantine, paté, ham mousse, veined Stilton cheese, Christmas pudding and mincemeat known to the buyer for a delicatessen.

Not content with all this, there are intricate patterns made of examples of many coloured marbles on the sides of the plinths of some of these statues, like pattern-books of stone.

The Great Dining-Room°

Answers perfectly, never feeling over large: it has got rather too compact a look; it is like dining in a great trunk, and you expect the lid to open. In this age of ornament and decoration the lines appear too straight. An easy remedy would be to add some scrolls to the picture-frames.

Here are the other columns from Richmond House. I don't know which Duke of Richmond imported, and then left them for so many years in their rotting cases: two are of the Breccia called Africano, and two are Porto Santo.

The Sculptors, Westmacott Son, and Sievier, made the chimney-pieces for me: they are clever and well executed, but do not nearly approach the idea I wished to see realized. I wanted more abandon, and joyous expression. I find these Baccanali too composed and sedate.

The Great Dining-Room

Figures by
Westmacott in the
Great Dining-Room:
'I wanted more
abandon'

The pictures here are very good : they deserve a better light, but that could not be obtained ; and for a place in such a room they must condescend to lose some advantage.

The four sideboards are slabs of great value. The red ones are from Sweden, a finer porphyry than that of Elvdalen, and those of slate-coloured Siberian Jasper are presents from the Emperor Nicolas. The two small tables were in the drawing-room at Wanstead ; their slabs of bianco e nero antico are veneered, which I did not mind in the days of that purchase. Admire the dado of Derbyshire marble, and my invention under the windows, of white marble, that prevents each weather-studier from leaving the traces of his well-blacked boots upon a wooden plinth.

The first dinner given in this room was for Queen Victoria, at the age of thirteen, when she came here with the Duchess of Kent (saying the first, I must add, that there had been a cooked rehearsal the day before). It was her first experience of a dinner with grown-up people.

181

Eleven years after, five only of the same party dined here—Herself, Lord Morpeth, Lord Waterpark, Sir Augustus Clifford, and I.

'Answers perfectly, never feeling over large.' I suppose size is a matter of what you are used to. I think most people would find this room very large indeed. It was eaten in until 1939. Its colour was dark sick, and dirty to boot. We did not attack it until 1963, when it was hung with oyster-coloured watered silk, the ceiling painted white (with too much pink in it—my fault) a ticklish job because of the delicacy of the gilding of the foliage in the ceiling and the way the paint and the gold meet.

I found the four big glass lights fixed to the wall in boxes in the stables. They were at Devonshire House. The glass arms which hold the candles are nearly the same pattern as those on the chandelier, so they fit in well. They replace the hunting-horn lights which are now on the West stairs. The curtains are of the same Indian silk as those in our dining-room.

It looks formal and fine when the table is laid for a phantom dinner party and the side tables are covered in silver, china, and queer pink Bohemian glass—all ready for the ghostly diners who never arrive.

At the entrance to this room I once heard a good strong Yorkshire voice say loudly over his shoulder to his wife who was dallying in the Ante-Library, 'Bigh, tea's laid Mabel.'

The Vestibule °

The Vestibule is well contrived, connected with the office staircase, and with spaces containing ovens, presses, and cupboards belonging to the dinner service. The spacious music gallery above has a totally separate staircase and communication, and nothing interrupts the view when the whole apartment is opened.

The two Indian idols were sent from Guzzerat by Lord Clare, whom I had requested to get me some specimens of native sculpture. The Burmese divinity was bought in London.

Here is the only object bought by my father-in-law, a model of a ship carved from bone by Napoleonic prisoners of war.

This is where the band played for the staff parties.

The Sculpture Gallery°

A great part of the new building was finished, and the space for this Gallery remained without any decision as to its decoration. A place that was to receive three of Canova's works excited grand ideas. One project was to line the walls with marble, another to floor it with Swedish porphyry: the first was overruled from finding that sculptors, and most people, considered the Chatsworth stone a better background for sculpture than any other material, and free from the disadvantage of reflected light, which would be produced by polished marble; and it was ascertained from Stockholm that the floor would have cost £1500 before it even left that city. The doorcases of Derbyshire marble, though of a kind used hitherto for common purposes, are very handsome on this scale, relieved by the beauty of the columns and their gold capitals.

My Gallery was intended for modern sculpture, and I have almost entirely abstained from mixing with it any fragments of antiquity: it was in vain to hope for time or opportunities of collecting really fine ancient marbles. In addition to the statues, my wish was to obtain specimens of all the rare coloured marbles as pedestals for them. Some persons think that the columns, vases, &c., should be removed, as diminishing the effect of the statues. It may be so, but I am too fond of them to make the change.

I was informed of the two large columns at the North end by Lord Stuart de Rothsay at Paris, and, accompanied by Lady Morley, went off to an obscure shop to inspect, and finding them handsome (though not rare, being of Verde d'Egitto, and modern) I bought and ordered capitals for them before the Gallery was designed, knowing that Sir Jeffry would be sure to adapt them well somewhere. The capitals are of the finest Or-moulu by Delafontaine, at Paris. The price he charged was enormous: he attempted to excuse it by proving how much more he had been paid for the capitals on the Arc de Triomphe in the Place du Carrousel. I know not quite what advantage we gained in having them as models for the capitals at the other end, and for the four semi-capitals which were made in Derbyshire, of cast iron; and you are not to be told the price, but I know that one of them, English, here, cost exactly a fifth of the French there.

The beautiful columns of this, the South end, single stones including their bases, were bought in London, Chantrey informing me of them: they were not dear at three hundred guineas, and what is curious is, that the two blocks of oriental porphyry, on which the magnificent pedestals of Canova's Hebe and the bust of Napoleon stand, were, in a rough unpolished state, thrown into the bargain on the purchase being made. These, and all the columns of ancient marble, were repolished at Ashford marble mills. The chandeliers were bought at Wanstead; they accord well with the capitals and other few gilded ornaments in the room. The eagles originally had snakes in their beaks, but that gave such offence, as an indignity to my crest, that I was compelled to remove the much respected reptiles, and make the eagles support the termination of their chains instead. I am now going to prose to you about my marbles, as considerately as I possibly can. We will begin with the South-west corner.

Kessel's Discobolus was very much approved of at Rome. He was a Flemish sculptor, and died soon after the completion of this work. He wrote me word of the present King of Prussia's great admiration of it. The bust in the circular niche was among the few marbles I inherited at Devonshire House. The small rocchio is of Egyptian breccia, which is the same substance as the Tomb of Alexander in the British Museum. You may remember the two vases of serpentine, of an unusual shape, over my Father's dining-room chimney at Devonshire House. The little table was made at Matlock: it contains bits of marble picked up by Mr. Paxton, when he travelled with me. You have already seen my own gleanings, (more numerous, because the toil of many journeys) in the pavement of the mineral room. The pedestal of the Discobolus contains a tour de force of the Swedish porphyry-cutters, sent me by the Directors of the works, to show how beautifully and minutely they could work those hard materials, and it is wonderful. The other side has a slab of an old table of Mostre, bought at Baldock's famous shop, recently closed.

Pietro Tenerani, pupil of Thorwaldsen, made me the wounded Venus: he had already finished one for Prince Nicolas Esterhazy. He has become very distinguished, and was for many years the finisher of Thorwaldsen's works.

The two columns supporting rough porphyry vases are of Derbyshire materials. We call one rosewood marble, and the other moss agate; but that, I think, is a flourish, and the slab in Trentanove's pedestal is rather more moss agate than the column. The bas-reliefs on each side of Thorwaldsen's Night are by the Prussian Rudolph Schadow: he died young. One of them was broken on the voyage. The bas-reliefs in this division of the room were first placed in the Orangery, which was finished many years before, but they were quite lost there, too high, and yet soon concealed by the growth of the trees.

The Sculpture Gallery

When I think of Schadow and Kessels, Canova and Thorwaldsen, and Chantrey, it seems to me that I am outliving all my sculptors, and that chiselling must be a short-lived occupation.

The oval bas-relief and its companion opposite were on each side of the fire place in the Library, and the little group of Amorini was actually in the chimneypiece, which was a patchwork affair. The brackets supporting the Burmese deity in the Vestibule formed part of it.

The beautiful bust of Cardinal Consalvi was a posthumous portrait of him done by Thorwaldsen from memory, and much assisted by Lawrence's sketch for his picture of the Cardinal; and there never was a more perfect likeness. The medallion above was in the closet of the Queen of Scot's apartment here, and was always called the Duke of Alva, to which neither you nor I have any objection.

Campbell took about fourteen years to complete the statue of the Princess Pauline Borghese: she sat repeatedly to him for the bust, and gave him casts of her hand, foot, and nose. She was no longer young, but retained the beauty and charm that made her brother strike the medal in honour of the Sister of the Graces. Campbell used to bring his modelling clay to a pavilion in the garden of her villa, close to the Porta Pia. It had a little door opening to the street, independent of the entrance, through which Jerome Bonaparte and his wife came to see the progress of the work. The Princesse de Montfort was a sister to the King of Wirtemberg, very like our royal family—mother to the charming Princesse Mathilde, who has married Anatole Dimidoff. The little luncheons on those occasions were delightful; for the Princess Borghese, when compelled not to talk about dress, was extremely entertaining, and full of the histories of her times.

Inserted in the pedestal of this statue are twenty-six medallions, curious from their history and their material, more than from any merit of execution. They were cast of the iron ore of Elba, by the order of Napoleon during his residence there: they accompanied him to St. Helena, and were left by him to his sister, who bequeathed them to me. There were twenty-eight; but I had a seal made of one, an Intaglio of the dying gladiator; and a profile, well remembered, of Pauline herself was missing in the case when it reached me.

Canova kept the large bust of Napoleon in his bed-room till his dying day. He finished it from the study of the colossal statue, now in the possession of the Duke of Wellington. Lady Abercorn, who was a great friend, bought it immediately after his death of the Abbate Canova, his brother, and left it by her will to me. I know of no other authentic bust of Napoleon by Canova;

and I believe that none exists, though everybody calls their own so. And now you must look under the bracket on your left hand for Canova's tools—another interesting relic procured by that warm-hearted friend of the great sculptor—and certainly the last he employed. Her sister, Lady Julia Lockwood, gave them to me. Lady Abercorn had the strongest feelings, and could not disguise them, or her grief at her friend's death; so that in Rome, that city of fountains, she was called from her ready tears the Acqua Infelice.

Madame Mère! first acquired treasure, next to Endymion the most valued! Renouard, a French bookseller, negotiated the purchase for me at Paris in 1818. Canova made no repetition of it; but, after his death, Jerome, Prince de Montfort, got Trentanove to copy the original cast in marble, and that or another copy saw I in Palazzo Bacciochi at Bologna. But Canova was truth, and he told me there was no other by him. The old lady herself used to receive me at Rome, and rather complained of my possessing her statue, though my belief is that it was sold for her advantage. Canova made it at Paris, and it was exhibited in the Louvre. Lord Holland found the single word that expresses so much on the pedestal—one Greek word from the Iliad, that says, "Unfortunate mother of the greatest of men."

The large head of Achilles was by a Mr. Rennie, studying at Rome: he has now, I understand, eschewed sculpture.

Gott's Musidora, near the warm air apparatus, appears to court the element of fire, rather than to prepare for plunging into the water. Westmacott's Cymbal-player is charming—his Bacchanti, in the pedestal, spirited enough this time. The rosso bas-reliefs were bought at Ignazio Vescovalis, at Rome, in 1839—whether old or new I know not, nor care much.

Gibson came to England, at last, this year, and chose the place for his bas-relief of Hero and Leander. In our early acquaintance he made a sketch of it in a small album:

*"In that dear embrace
Soul has rushed forth to soul."*

Bartolini kept me waiting, not impatiently, year after year for his nymph. I had not the opinion of her at the beginning that I have now. She is a lovely and successful production of art.

The Lions give but a faint idea of the astonishing nature and effect of Canova's, by the tomb of Clement the Fourteenth, in St. Peter's. The sleep-

ing one sees: it was worked by Rinaldi; the other by Francesco Benaglia.

Pozzi, who has since removed to Florence, his country, where he has made great progress, made the group of Latona. She has got her enemies besides the Shepherds: the young Diana bored amused me.

The round bas-relief of the fall of Manna in the Wilderness was placed over the chimney in the old breakfast-room, in a carved wooden frame of strawberry leaves, now sent, with many other things, to the ceiling of the ball-room.

The double head of Isis and Serapis is a copy done at Rome in Ashford marble of the beautiful basalt original found at the Villa Adriana, and now in the Museum of the Capitol. It got damaged here. Certain actors of charades, classically desirous of illustrating the syllable Nile in Kenilworth, knocked off a horn, and damaged some other part; and in vain, the Gods being found too heavy to go in procession.

Schadow's Filatrice made his fortune, and was often repeated.

Carlo Finelli was greatly praised by Canova, and the finish of his Cupid and Psyche approaches that of his great master's works.—"Where's Psyche?" why, in Cupid's hands.

Hebe came on springs by post from Wales, and Allan Cunningham, foreman, sculptor, poet, placed her behind my seat in the old dining-room, where, on her removal, it felt strange to have a meal without her.

Canova's bust of Madonna Laura was dearly loved by the sculptor, entirely formed by his own chisel; and it required all the Duchess of Devonshire's powers of persuasion, added to my entreaties, to make him part with her. The other four small busts are not very remarkable. The Ceres is pretty, worked by Rinaldi from the block without a model: he modestly charged only fifty crowns for it. The vestal was copied from Canova by Trentanove.

Thorwaldsen's Venus is a perfectly beautiful woman—not at all Goddess. She arrived broken in three places; and here friend Allan Cunningham, sent by Chantrey to repair her, was of the greatest advantage. It was a delicate operation, and pins of brass were inserted to make the restoration secure, and the work has stood several removals. A bracelet, hiding the fracture of the arm, is one that the Princess Pauline procured when she went into mourning on the death of Napoleon, and she gave it me for this object. The bas-reliefs by the great Scandinavian were made for Agar Ellis, who transferred his purchase to me: I know few things more beautiful.

The small oval bas-relief was between the windows of the old breakfast-

room. *If you will examine the vase of Alabastro Cotognino, you will know what wonderful beauty and effect columns, at least as large as those of the doorcases here, must have.*

The Ganymede and Eagle are by Tadolini. The pale Cipollino column was brought home by the Black Rod, who, when afloat, made ballast of all goods he thought would suit me. The vase of Africano is too fat. Lord Ashley gave me the white round slab, a slice of one of the signal columns on the Promontory of Sunium, of which I possess so splendid a share in the pleasure-ground. There is the bust of a Bacchante by Gott in the circular niche, which reminds me that I passed over his lovely group of greyhounds. He is the Landseer of marble.

And now we come to Gibson's Mars—a group of great effect and admirable work. My knowing Gibson was entirely owing to Canova, who was the most generous and liberal of men to the rising artists of his day. You have seen many of Gibson's works at Rome; and his zephyr-carried Psyche, judging by the bronze representation of it on a small scale here, must be perfectly beautiful.

I conclude with Endymion.

If evidence were wanting of its having been finished by Canova, I have plenty of letters in my possession that establish that point; but none can be required when you contemplate the admirable perfection of the work. The quality of the marble is so fine, so hard, so crystalline, that Canova would not change it on account of the stain in the arm; that on the cheek he liked, and thought it represented the sunburnt hunter's hue. He had often inquired of me what subject I preferred, and which of his works, and I told him always the sleeping Genius of the Archduchess Christine's tomb at Vienna, and also the Genius on Rezzonico's monument. He accordingly promised me something that I should like still better. I had really attached myself to him very much; and it was with mingled feelings of grief and exultation, of boundless admiration and recent bereavement, that I first saw my group in the well-known studio, where I had passed so many happy hours with the most talented, the most simple, and most noble-minded of mankind.

What anxiety for its voyage to England! A cast of it, sent from Leghorn to Havre, was lost at sea: it was to have been copied in bronze at Paris. In other respects, good fortune has attended all my cargoes; and the contents of this room afford me great satisfaction and pleasure, and are among the excuses for an extravagance that I can neither deny nor justify, nor (when I look at Endymion) repent.

Of all the rooms in the house this is the one which underlines changing taste the most. Mr Thompson, writing in 1951, dismisses it thus; 'Pure Wyatville again and, except for the bas-reliefs from the present library inlaid in the projecting walls, entirely filled with examples of the work of sculptors (Canova, Thorvaldsen, Gibson, Campbell, etc.) popular in the 6th Duke's time but now generally despised. Most noteworthy, or least unnoteworthy, among these are Canova's head of Napoleon,* the seated statue of Napoleon's mother, and his recumbent Endymion, the latter a lovely piece of marble, if nothing more.'

Granny disliked it all and even put the recumbent lions outside to take their chance in the garden. The Bachelor Duke's statues, which he took such trouble to get and which pleased him so enormously, were looked upon as so much bulky trash for eighty or ninety years.

Suddenly, in the last ten years, the vast portraits are admired again, much spoken of, borrowed for exhibitions, and revered as great works of art.

I think the Sculpture Gallery is a very successful room. The proportions are good and contain the giant heads of Canova and Rennie as though they were life-size.

It is lit from above, so you are denied the temptation of looking out, which concentrates the mind on the things displayed and makes it a good place to show manuscripts, maps, letters and any other smaller objects, in big glass cases.

The two massive gilt gasoliers from Wanstead hang from the ceiling, now electrified.

The quiet Victorian faces of virginal girls gaze past the naked bodies of Discobolus, Achilles, Ganymede and Endymion as if they weren't there. Napoleon's mother and sister sit on their white marble chairs either side of the Tsar's huge malachite clock, and in a niche high above the oddly assembled company is the benign face of the Bachelor Duke himself.

In the early 1960s I put the red velvet hangings on the walls of two-thirds of the room and green velvet at the end, to relieve the everlasting stone colour. A traveller to Russia told me she saw sculptures there placed in front of brightly painted stone walls and how well they looked. I thought that to paint the walls would be too drastic in case the next

*See illustration on page 159

Bust of the Bachelor
Duke in the
Sculpture Gallery

generation disliked it, so I hung the coloured stuff instead. The
Solymossy sisters made it, helped by the daily ladies.

Note the door-stops: sawn-off models of the Great Conservatory.

The Orangery°

*Here happened one of the few deviations, in Sir Jeffry Wyatville's progress,
from his first intentions, that occurred during the progress of the works. The
suite of rooms was to have ended with the Statue Gallery. The place of
honour for the finest work I might obtain was to have been in the centre,
where the door now opens into this place. Talk there was about the great
weight of statues and other works to be brought in, and a process was to be
contrived for raising them by pullies from the carriage-way below—all which
has been proved to be quite unnecessary. The front of the office bedrooms was
actually built; a covered passage, open to the east, was to lead from a door on
the right to the basement of the Banquetting, or Ball-room building: there is
in one of the turrets a model showing how all this was to be. In the meantime,*

191

however, I got bit by gardening; and though I had before, as a matter of ornament, wished to have a conservatory in some way connected with the great apartment, I did not till 1827 add the alteration now spoken of to the plan. Sir Jeffry, on my wish being expressed, made no difficulty in the execution: the East windows of the new building were condemned, and converted—the upper ones into niches, and the lower into flower-baskets. It was lucky that only two rooms were sacrificed by the change: a lofty space was gained, the morning sun, and an immense addition to the effect of the suite of rooms. I cannot help being over-candid, and telling you what otherwise you would hardly discover. It is that great error occurred here, how or why I find it hard to understand; but I suppose the external elevation could not be made to agree with that of the front of the office building—so that the middle folding-door is not true to the middle window, or niche, of the superseded front. The difference is not great, but it entailed another result out of doors, that has the appearance, and indeed the reality, of still greater irregularity. It will be time to talk of this when we are in the pleasure-ground. The wish to adapt the old greenhouse on the hill to stove plants made me urge the finishing of this place long before the rest of the house. It was accordingly completed; and impatient to see the effect of Thorwaldsen and Schadow's bas-reliefs in a good light, I placed them here, where you see the six mouldings that surrounded them. Cincinnato Baruzzi's group of Venus and Cupid was also placed in one of the niches: he was a clever sculptor, a pupil of Canova's. He had very great success at first, and a nymph of his for Lord Kinnaird, repeated for Lord George Cavendish, was deservedly admired, and made his early reputation. He was over-anxious to please me, and modelled too fast, and the result has not satisfied, and remains only on the threshold of my collection. In 1841 I found Baruzzi established at the Studii, or Museum, at Bologna, under the same roof, and apparently prosperous.

Bartolini copied the Medicis Vase for me with great care. At first it was in the Gallery, then was ordered to the pleasure-ground, when I fell to bedecking that region with white marble; but, being wheeled thus far on its way, the effect was so beautiful under orange and araucaria, that it stopped short, and here remains. Of a night it holds powerful lamps, that send up such a magical light on the branches of the Altingia, that people cry out Fairy land.

Among the orange trees here, four came from the Empress Josephine's collection at Malmaison. I believe they are the only survivors, for Lord

The Shop in the
Orangery

Ailsa's and Lord Aylesbury's died, and Lord Londonderry's were burnt.
The Rhododendron Arboreum was one of those that first astonished the
world at Knight's Nursery garden in the King's Road: I was obliged to give
£50 in order to possess it here. The poor tree now looks consumptive and
worn-out, from having been allowed to flower beyond its strength. The
Altingia Excelsa was the first I obtained: it was a rare plant when I gave
Lowe, of Clapton, a sum for it nearly as large as the Rhododendron price.
On arriving it was put into the Berlin granite tazza, which then stood in the
middle of this Orangery: it has been a traveller in its youth, and somehow
returned from Petersburg, and was exchanged with Lowe for other plants.
The admiration for these plants has since caused their introduction in great
numbers. By the kindness of Mr. J. Payne Collier, I obtained a large box,
full of young plants, from his friend the Chief Justice of New South Wales at
Sydney. They never will endure the frosts of our climate, and their rapid
growth within doors allows few greenhouses to show them to advantage: the
heat of a stove weakens their growth, but with common protection nothing
seems to disagree with them; and here are two branches of the same plant
that thrive and flourish in the most eccentric manner, one with all the
appearance and luxuriance of a tree, but obstinately refusing to form a
leader; the other, a cutting from it, as pendulous as ivy. The orange trees
remain here almost always in good health and condition, perfuming the
whole of Chatsworth with their blossoms.

The last room of the tour of the house has been turned into a monument
to my passion for commerce. It is a shop run on the lines recommended
forcefully in Beatrix Potter's *Ginger and Pickles*, a cautionary tale of a

village shop and surely the best book on retailing ever written. Admittedly there are a number of things here which are not for sale. The coach, the giant piece of quartz found when the Simplon Pass was made, the Bartolini copy of the Medici Vase, the glass shades of the hanging lamps, and more statues and urns of massive Chatsworth proportions.

The coach was brought here in the 1890s by Louise Duchess. We went to the Coronation of 1953 in it. It travelled to London by train, accompanied by two stout grey horses from the Matlock riding school, which were stabled at Watney's Brewery.

On that cold, wet, June morning, we trundled slowly from our house in Chesterfield Street round Hyde Park Corner to Piccadilly, where we waited for the Duke of Wellington to join us from Apsley House, and turned down St. James's Street, where we were passed by Lord Bath, alone in his elegant yellow coach drawn by a pair of Hackneys which trotted by as if we were standing still. Our driver did not know London and got lost somewhere behind the Army & Navy Stores. It was an awful moment, as we had to be in the Abbey in good time because Sto, aged nine, was page to my mother-in-law, who was Mistress of the Robes to the Queen. The only communication with the coachman was a piece of string attached to a button on his coat, but however desperately the string was pulled, it could not give a message, so Andrew had to put his head out of the window (made of thin, real glass) and shout instructions, to the amusement of the crowds. There is surprisingly little room inside, and two grown-ups and a boy of nine filled it completely. The two men in family livery standing behind were from the Chatsworth farm and knew London not at all. One of them, in charge of the Jersey herd, said to me as I was getting into the coach, loaded down by ermine, velvet and tiara, 'Marigold had a cow calf yesterday' —a proper reminder of real life going on at home.

When the Orangery was first arranged as a shop, the stalls stood in a circle round the giant vase, and it was extremely pretty. The crowds of people and the unexpected success of our wares has made it much bigger now, and the selling part takes nearly all the space.

Here ends the tour of the house and the visitor is spat out into the garden whether it is wet or fine. But you, poor reader, must brace yourself, because we still have to look at the Baths, the Theatre (or Ball Room), the Offices, the Cellars and the Roof, before going out of doors to the Stables, and thence to the Pleasure Grounds for a two-mile walk.

The Baths*

I am going to show you the Baths before we go up-stairs to the Ball-room:

The two smaller baths are convenient, and much frequented when I have company. The other is the most luxurious and enjoyable one that I know. The water of it is heated by retorts over the fire in a vault underneath, from which it is conveyed by a slanting pipe to the coiled pipes, that fill the entire space under the perforated tiles of the floor, by which the water is circulated and cooled to the temperature required. By this contrivance steam in the bath is avoided.

The baths still exist and are a store in the night-watchman's flat.

The Theatre (Ball Room) '

Now for the Ball-room, by some called Banquetting-Room—or better, the room to make a row in. It is especially the theatre of Charades.

Till the Queen's visit, the panels were in the ceiling without any connecting ornament: Mr. Crace added the whole of the enriched part on that occasion. Sir James Thornhill was the painter of Andromeda, who used to sprawl on the north side of the centre room in the West front. The six largest panels were in the Library; the intermediate landscapes came from other parts of the house. You will easily distinguish the modern foliage and masks by the infinitely superior execution of the old ones. The panels from the old billiard-room are over the Gallery.

The private boxes look very well when inhabited, and full of people and whist-tables; and when the Duke of Sussex was in one, with his cap on, looking like a Doge, the whole thing seemed as if painted by Paul Delaroche. At the Queen's ball, a platform was raised for her at the West side, and the window was suppressed, the recess being filled with drapery of white tissu de verre. I have forgotten the name of the Berlin artist who made the chandelier: he obtained the horns, and permission to employ them, from the late King. The winter decoration here, of rich colour, with folds or columns of velvet, looked extremely well.

Having got thus far, and not to make you climb again, we will now go into the temple attic, called by Lady Wharncliffe the Poussin. The idea of it was mine: it was suggested to me at Oxford by the tower of the Schools, which forms part of the Bodleian, where the five orders of architecture rise above each other.

Sir Jeffry Wyatville had not intended to build anything above the Ball-room, but readily adopted my plan. The views of the neighbouring country through the Corinthian columns have a beautiful effect: Sir Thomas Lawrence employed Mr. Cowen to draw them; I obtained one of his best views, and almost regret that Queen Adelaide's admiration of it at Brighton made me give it to her.

For some years after we came to live here the Theatre was a store and had the depressing smell and feeling of a place which is locked and dead except to searchers for forgotten furniture. It was very dirty as well, from years of neglect. In the early sixties we covered the walls with red rep and hung curtains of red velveteen and blue silk lining, trimmed with bobbles dyed in tea to correspond with the painted curtains framing the stage—all made by Miss Feeney, of course.

The two backdrops, which let down by a complicated series of pulleys, are a desert island and a drawing-room, which presumably cover all possibilities known to theatre. There is a trap-door in the stage for devils to come up or down according to the piece. As I am a complete failure when it comes to entertainment before footlights, this pretty theatre has never been used for the purpose for which it was intended, except for a memorable concert given to inaugurate a local orchestra. Every seat was occupied, but mostly by people who were unpractised in the art of listening to music, and there was clapping when there should not have been at those false stops between movements when the unwary wake up and clap out of good manners.

The Temple Attic or Belvedere above would most probably have been pulled down by my father-in-law but for the outbreak of war in 1939.

The Theatre with its scenery

The Offices°

East Lobby. This, with another part since pulled down, used to be the servants' hall, and a very bad one: it is now chiefly used as a passage in which you must be skilful to avoid falling over all those trunks. On the left hand are the House-keepers' private apartments, consisting of three rooms that were the tea-room and the footmen's rooms. The sitting-room is very good, though not quite so much so as a friend thought, when he said to me, "You know your mother had not such a room as this." It is, however, convenient and light, and overlooks all arrivals: there hangs my picture, by Ellerby, who is become the painter of the Peak. Next to these, towards the

North, comes the servants' hall, a beautiful example of Sir Jeffry's stone-work, arched, as the Offices chiefly are, with great solidity and strength.

We now cross the Office-passage towards the kitchen, through a court in which you may observe the apparatus of a jack turned by water. The kitchen itself is handsome and spacious, and contains steam-cupboards, and a hot steam-table; and wood is the sole fuel employed in the huge grate, as well as coke for the steam contrivances, which, diminishing the quantity of blacks, must add greatly to the cleanliness of the place. There is a good arrangement for preserving the fish alive in water, till the moment of execution. The pastry convenient, the scullery awful, and the larder atrocious; for, although it may be airy, and highly convenient for salting, it looks into the abysses of a dusty coal-yard. My cook, Mr. Howard, ought to be the best in the world; for thirty years ago, when at Paris, I modestly requested Louis XVIII. to place him in his kitchen, to which his Majesty immediately consented for some months: and it was kind of the lately restored Monarch, at a moment when many thought him in constant danger of poison; but he was gracious to me, and always said "Duc, c'est l'air natal que vous respirez." Mr. Howard studied also at Robert's and Very's. I spare you bakehouse, washhouse, and laundry: neither will we boast of the poultry-yard; but the dairy, of good architecture, is not bad. You pass under a building that contains the Clerk of the works' office and lodging-rooms, and by a gun-room to the Porter's lodge, in the more distant part of which is a collection of ancient fragments.

You will be dead tired by now and have a bad attack of visual indigestion so I will let you off what the Bachelor Duke calls the offices and the Bachelor Bedrooms, areas of rooms called the Birds, California, the Four Score Attics, the East Attics, Kitchen, Still Room, Pantry, the Vegetable Rooms, a passage full of huge 1930s refrigerators (welcomed by Mrs Tanner because the ice cut from the canal and stored in the ice-house there was 'full of swan's dirt'), the Copper Store, Muniment Room, offices of the Librarians and Comptroller, the Telephone Exchange, the Lamp Room, Carpenters' Shop, the Kitchen Maids' rooms (which house not kitchen maids, alas, but braid and tassels, cushions and curtains, coal-scuttles and fire-irons from abandoned houses), while in the attics are bedheads, flower vases, mattresses piled on top of one another like an illustration from the Princess and the Pea, books four deep on temporary shelves, colza oil lamps and, here and there, bicycles, skates, cricket bats, and croquet mallets. There is the Sewing Room, the old Laundry stuffed with boxes full of brittle and filthy papers to do with the estate and estates long since sold, bits of chandeliers, tin boxes of peculiar shapes containing military hats of vanished regiments, and the Paint Room where there is a lump on one wall where colour after colour has been tried till it sticks out in a fat bulge, several inches of solid paint. I often think that many of the people who come round the house would like to see how it works, and I am quite sure most of the men would be far more interested in the boilers and the coke mountain than the State Rooms, and the women would 'Oo' and 'Ah' over the old vegetable preparation rooms, the Scullery, the spits, the china and linen cupboards and silver safe. They would be surprised to see the contents of one long cupboard which holds a hoard of torn napkins, and another occupied by lids belonging to china dishes broken long ago.

They might even like to see the five separate cellars, stone floors, walls, roofs and ceilings, which run under all the house. Or they might be like some friends who had 'done' the whole of Hardwick with Granny as enthusiastic guide, and when they got back to their starting-point and their feet were finished and their brains nigh on addled, were horror-struck to hear her say brightly, 'Now I expect you would like to see the cellars?' 'I think I shall *die* if I have to see the cellars,' the bravest answered. They were never asked to Hardwick again.

Nevertheless, in the hope that the reader will survive it we must go down into the cellar at Chatsworth.

The Cellar•

To that cellar we now descend to look at the twelve Apostles, once a great lion, being oaken butts, with the first Duke's arms carved upon them, and said to have been a present to him from King William III. The four Judges are plain, and so are the twelve Jurymen. The wine-cellar is insignificant; the beer-cellars an endless labyrinth. The beer, brewed above the stables, is conveyed to the cellars by a pipe under ground, 1059 feet long, of three inch bore, the idea of which always gives me a longing, on some great occasion, to form a fountain of that liquid.

The Cellar

Beer was home-brewed till 1898. The underground lead pipe skirted the gardeners' messhouse and when the beer was running through they used to drill a hole in it and get a length of copper tube with a loop on top and fill their cans.

After 1898 the beer was brought from a brewery. Till 1914 it was drunk by men and women servants for breakfast, at ten o'clock, for lunch, at tea-time and at six o'clock. Tradesmen, postmen and anyone who brought messages or parcels, no matter what time of day, went to the Servants' Hall for beer.

The Roof •

To refresh ourselves, we will now go up to the other extreme, the roof of the house. In doing so, we mount the least sightly staircase of all; but we avoid the four score and four, that dark ladder leading to the servants' rooms, a suite towards the East, with one room to the North, entirely occupied by livery servants. The others are lodged in attics to the North of the quadrangle, and above the new range of buildings. There is a communication at the head of the North stairs, and there you pass a room made memorable

*by the suicide of an unfortunate valet de chambre of Colonel Peel, who shot
himself there with his master's gun in consequence of bad luck at Doncaster.
It threw a gloom over the enjoyment of a large, gay party here. Near the door
hangs in a frame a curiosity from Raratonga; paper, but unlike paper,
paint, but unlike paint, the work of savages, and made by them for the
missionary Williams, who presented it to me here with other articles of their
work. He passed some days here with his wife and son: there was a great
charm in the simplicity of his character, his unaffected piety and
disinterestedness, and his courageous confidence of protection in the perilous
life he was about to encounter. His son had a turn for botany, and they took
out many plants that we thought would answer in the regions to which they
were bound. The tragical fate of poor Williams is well known.**

*Now we arrive at the leads; and for years I have not been there, not even
to see the new fountain to advantage, but the views are beautiful, and the
access to each front convenient and safe. In youth it was my constant practice
to bring people here, and also to run up the pediment, and sit for hours in
front of Minerva, at her feet reading, but not the book of wisdom, and
thinking those timid who would not accompany me to that pinnacle. That is
forty years ago, and now I should be sorry to attempt the flight.*

Vertigo prevents me from going on the roof, and I am ashamed to say
that when there was a fire in the North Attics in 1980, luckily discovered
and contained before too much damage was done, I watched from the
safety of the Chapel Passage. There was an immediate response to the
fire siren by scores of people from around about who had nothing to do
with the house. The house staff, helped by the volunteers, worked without
stopping till hundreds of books and the pictures and furniture within
range were moved to safety. A great deal of water was used to put out the
fire as the immense oak beams under the roof were well alight. It poured
down the walls to the ground floor, and I have an abiding memory of Dick
Norris, head keeper, an outdoor man more accustomed to giving orders
than receiving them, issued with a small housemaid's mop and mopping
far into the night as if it was his normal and favourite occupation.

The firemen and the helpers hurried to and fro on the leads protected
by the parapet all that long May evening, dragging the hose-pipes

*It was recent news when the Bachelor Duke was writing. John Williams was killed and
eaten at Erromanga in the New Hebrides in November 1839 'in retaliation, it is believed,
for the cruelties previously perpetrated by an English crew'.

about, playing water on the burning beams. It was a sombre warning of how disastrous a fire could be if it took hold in a more vulnerable part of the house. The only casualty was the chef, one of the first to discover the blaze, who cut his thumb breaking through a window and was taken to hospital to have it stitched, his white clothes smothered in blood as if he had been butchering a hapless pig.

The Stables°

These have been unaltered by me: they were built by my grandfather. They contain about eighty stalls for horses. In the days of breeding, training, &c., there were accommodations suitable to each department, neglected in these degenerate times. The place for exercise under cover is inconvenient from its square form, and not comparable to the colonnade at Buxton. I have added a new coach-house, to shelter the carriages of my visitors from the elements, to which they were exposed while standing and encumbering the said thoroughfare. I have always admired the exterior of the building, and fancied something Florentine in the character of its architecture.

The Stables were built by James Paine (1716–1789). Some of the eighty stalls are unchanged. Some have been turned into loose-boxes, two ranges are stores, and two are arranged for tea-drinkers instead of horses. Seats line the divisions of the stalls, which are marked by the hooves of generations of horses irritated by their strappers.

The carriage horses were hired at a pound a week each in the early 1900s, as it was not thought worthwhile to keep them all the year round when the Duke was only at Chatsworth for short periods. Some of their names are above the mangers.

The Granary above the south side of the square still holds exciting relics, from gilt and painted pelmets to unidentifiable rubbish. The rest of the top floor is flats, all occupied. On a bedroom door of one of them is painted 'Third Postilion'.

The Pleasure Grounds°

Emerging from the South-west end of the Stables, you find yourself in the midst of plants. The South front of the building used to be overgrown with trees, dark and damp: on clearing them away, the wall was found excellent for the growth of half hardy plants. A yellow China rose has braved many winters. Wistaria consequana and Magnolia conspicua are magnificent, the latter the finest I know. The growth of what was planted here, where there is no artificial heat, gave rise to the formation of the hot wall, containing flues, and protected by curtains during the winter, the success of which has been complete. Descending by it, you come to Flora's temple, which used to look upon a swamp, with the smoky roof of the old offices to the right, and my first improvement at Chatsworth, of which I was not a little proud, a wooden covered walk from house to stables, which it reached by winding through a damp sunk fence. It was demolished by greater works, and it would appear that we no longer care about wet clothes. Sir Jeffry Wyatville's first great hit out of doors was the invention of the broad gravel walk that is of so much use and ornament here.

The four columns in the middle were open, and a door between two seats led to the brick-walled kitchen-garden behind. The two sides contained orange-trees: they were converted into my first stove by Mr. Paxton, and now since the building of the great Conservatory, their climate has again become temperate, for the growth of camellias alone. Oh, days of childhood! here bided old John Barton, under-gardener, in his blue apron, who made us small hand fishingnets, and was famous for his translation of Cavendo Tutus, the motto on the South Front, when questioned by the bands of rustic sight-seers. But John Barton served under Mr. Travis, who was quite a different sort of person, and not so attractive to the young; prolix, old school, and very consequential, in a cocked hat and striped stockings, and gold shoe-buckles, wearing powder and a long pigtail—I am sure of the pigtail. Still, it was impossible not to be amused with his favourite story about the King of Denmark, the son-in-law, I suppose, of George II., who made a tour in England, and appears to have been un roi sans gêne. The King of Denmark, as Mr. Travis related, came to see Chatsworth in the absence of the family, but many of the neighbouring gentry and others were assembled on the lawn, in the hope of contemplating Majesty at the windows. In this they were soon more than gratified; for, having come out upon the steps, to Mr. Travis's amazement, the Majesty of Denmark walked down them, and did——but as to telling you what he did, that is quite impossible.

The parterre before the greenhouse was laid out in 1812. The cistern, now holding flowers instead of water, was, as I have said before, in the inner court, from whence also come the columns that supported the corridors. Here is Flora, promoted from the temple, and here are two statues in red and black granite from the great temple of Carnac, sent home by a famous traveller, and purchased by me in the New Road. The white cistern comes from Carrara. Remark the gold ornament inserted in the centre compartment of the frieze, above the columns: it is rather curious, having been in front of the car to which the Venetian horses were attached above the triumphal arch in the Place du Carrousel. On the day of their removal, in 1815, Sir George Hayter, who witnessed it, obtained this morsel of gilt lead, that for a few years had figured in so grand a situation. At what parades it has assisted, especially during the cent jours! what previous insults it witnessed, when, alluding to the empty vehicle, the fickle and ungrateful race below cried out—"Le char l'attend!" The painter brought me the trophy home.

Returning down the steps, we come by the broad walk to another flight of steps, built by me, which, with the long slope, replaces a deep wall or sunk fence, extending as far as the lower gravel walk, which was not there, now does. From below, it was unsightly; from above, so imperceptible, that a race down the hill is talked of between Charles Fox and Lord John Townshend, in which the former, unconscious of the wall, yet unable to stop in time, came down and broke his leg. A much steeper flight of steps nearer the windows, and containing a sort of water-temple, stood in the place of the present easy flight.

The garden is very big. It occupies 105 acres and the wall around it is nearly two miles long. The shape of it now is much the same as described in the Handbook. The greatest change is the disappearance of one big greenhouse and the appearance of another. The Great Conservatory is no more, but a successor to it was built in 1970 to a design by George Pearce after his magnificent greenhouse on two levels in the Edinburgh Botanic Gardens. I think it is beautiful—some people do not. 'This is the monstrosity I told you about,' I heard a woman say to her friend.

The site it occupies was a dank and dreary shrubbery of evergreens backing on to the old lean-to mess house behind the Camellia House. It has three climates—tropical, mediterranean and temperate. There are

The First Duke's Greenhouse, called the Camellia House

no inside supports for the roof, and the divisions are there to contain the temperatures. In the tropical garden there is a pool for the *Victoria regia* lily. This astonishing plant is an annual, grown from seed each year, and as the days lengthen the leaves grow to their full size, giant green saucers with turned up rims. Joseph Paxton was the first to introduce the lily, discovered in British Guiana in 1836, to this country, and he persuaded it to flower in a house built for it in the old kitchen garden at Barbrook in 1849. Other plants which thrive in the hot end are bananas (*Musa cavendishii*) which bear fruit, pineapples *Stephanotis*, *Jasminum rex*, *Passiflora quadrangularis* and *Passiflora* 'Empress Eugenie', *Pamianthe peruviana*, *Hedychium*, Eucharist lilies, papyrus, frangipani and, best of all, pawpaw. The middle section grows oranges, lemons, limes, daturas and night-flowering cactus (*Cactus grandiflorus* or the night-blowing cereus) which only flowers in the hours of darkness, and is well worth the walk out to see and smell at dusk on a summer evening when it has forty or fifty flowers, each lasting just one night and all dead in the morning.

In the temperate end are fruit trees, geraniums, camellias and an archway of fuchsias, as well as parsley and sorrel (I prefer plants to eat than to look at).

The earth for all this planting was dug from near the river in the park. It is alluvial sandy loam and has benefited from centuries of carrying cattle and sheep and being flooded in the winter.

The iron snakes and dates over the doors at each end were made by Bob Hutchinson, Chatsworth blacksmith.

The walls containing the terrace below are built of stone which was the base of the old orchid houses next to the vinery. When these were pulled down to make way for the less pretty but more practical greenhouse in 1969 the stones were sawn in half, thus doubling the quantity and revealing new surfaces and the grain of the local sandstone. We opened the way through the Camellia House (it has been enclosed by glass on the south side and the doorway to the north was filled in) and made a terrace of brick with a pebble star.

The scheme was completed in 1974 when the lower terrace was made. We left a holly and a yew and arranged the brick, kilned at Chatsworth in 1840, round them. The stone pavers making the circle were salvaged from Paxton's old Lily House where they had formed the rim of the pond.

The snake is the Cavendish family crest. Here it is made of pebbles from the Crumbles beach at Eastbourne. The cushion on which it rests is black and ruby red marble from Ashford-in-the-Water. The terrace was designed by Dennis Fisher (comptroller 1962–1979) and contructed by Malcolm Sellors. A laburnum tunnel flanking new steps in line with the middle of Paxton's 'Conservative Wall' is the final embellishment to this hitherto unsatisfactory part of the garden.

The Conservative Wall, or 'The Case', as it is always called, is the last important building by Paxton left in the garden. The scalloped wooden fringe of its roof was the fore-runner of many a station roof designed by Paxton when he was occupied with the railways. In the middle are two enormous *Camellia reticulata*, Captain Rawes variety, which are smothered in deep pink flowers with wavy petals and golden stamens in March and April. It is thought that Paxton planted them in the 1850s.

Paxton's 'Conservative Wall'

Now their trunks measure two feet three inches round at three feet high.

The Vine House produces Muscat grapes (planted in 1921) of rare quality from August to January. The 'parterre before the greenhouse' is a rose garden now.

The borders leading from the Orangery towards the greenhouses are planted in blue and white colours and in those over the main gravel path between the pollarded oaks all the flowers are yellow, orange and red. Cecil Beaton came to stay when the borders were flowering in these colours for the first time and as we walked along the gravel path and the brilliant hot colours came into view I said, 'What do you think of this?' hoping for some sort of praise. What a hope! He was really shocked by it, and said in his most exaggerated voice, '*Eow* it's too *arful!* It's a *retina irritant.*'

The South Front°

You are now before the South Front, where I like to think that what I have done for embellishment and ornament is in the spirit of the design carried out by the first Duke. The sculptor, Cibber, was, I find, employed in the pleasure-ground from 1687 till 1691.

Cibber made the Triton fountain in 1688. He was succeeded by Jan Thomas Geeraertson, who worked the sea nymphs at the cascade-temple, and Edmond Pearman, and they were employed till 1693. The marble basin for the inner court, mentioned above, was not built till 1698, and cost £60. The terrace wall and stairs in the West Front were built in 1697. Altogether, these sculptors seem to have received not more than £500.

I have agreements, signed by the first Duke and his gardener, George London, concerning the laying-out of the grounds, their turfing, planting, and gravelling, dated August, 1688, which, with many other documents, show that great numbers of persons were employed in that eventful year.

I must not, however, allow these details to engross our attention too much, my plan being, in the garden as it was in the house, to act as showman to you; and now, in this South front, you perceive that its architecture remains unaltered, except that the steps are wholly rebuilt, containing nothing of the old materials but the two keystones, on which fanciful heads were carved, probably by Cibber, one of a satyr, and the other as like as if it had been intended for the portrait of a Lady Jane Montague, whose early death we lamented in our youth; and having passed these, you see that the thickness of the Chapel walls has permitted recesses to be made deep enough to afford shelter from sun and rain: these recesses contain seats, and the place has altogether obtained the name of Granville Corner.

What happy, and never to be forgotten times ran their peaceful course here!

I had better separate what is old from what is new. The temple-cascade is old, but the gravel walk leading up to it is new; and when the two lines met, to the dismay of all beholders, an elbow, or long angle, presented itself to the eye, making it necessary to take up more than half the flight of water-covered steps, and replace them true to the lines of the South Front, and, consequently, to those of the gravel walk. They ceased to be true to their own temple, but no eye can detect that, whereas the deviation outraged the most careless glance. It is not easy to say why the irregularity existed, whether it arose originally from bad measurement, or from the design of showing the cascade more fully to lookers-out of the window. — To resume, the cascade is old, the tunnel under it the newest of the new, contrived to hide the march of coal-carts conveying fuel to the great Conservatory.

Robinhood's stone is old, but the cataract over it is new : that water should come down the hill is old — that it should be visible is new. The eternal hills are clothed by trees and groves that have sprung up since Chatsworth was built ; the writers of that day record the contrast of the house with its "bleak and horrid situation." It is new to see the Queen's rock peeping through the glade, the sun's rays reflected from the glass of the Conservatory, a "temple through the dark wood shining." The small fountain, Triton and his horses, the great fountain and its river-gods, are old : the streams they vomit forth are fresh supplies, and the Emperor fountain is the spirit of novelty, dashing its endless variety to the skies.

Eight statues and two vases have been worked for me by Francesco Bienaimé at Carrara, of hard marble of that place, that appears to defy the climate of the Peak, and to resist all incipient vegetation on its surface. I think them a great addition ; the eye reposes with pleasure on those classic forms. The bronze Endymion was worked by Chantrey from a cast made at Rome : it appears to me that the art of casting bronze fit to endure our climate is unknown in England. The venerable balustrade on the right hand must be older than the house ; I brought it to light from the almost total concealment in which a cut holly hedge enveloped it. The hedge was rather a loss, but it is well replaced by trained Pyracanthus.

Beyond the balustrade is the row of lime trees called Dr. Johnson's walk : he sat and discoursed under their shade after dining here in the summer of 1784.

Between the statues on the south lawn till 1952 were eight raised beds supported by tufa rock and containing thin pink Poulsen roses. I thought they were out of scale and out of keeping, so I replaced them with double rows of pleached limes (*Tilia platyphyllos rubra*) in 1952. Like all new planting in a place of such size and importance, they looked ridiculous, no more than threads, for years. Their wooden supports, much bigger than the limes themselves, and the wires they were to be trained along, looked like pylons. It took about fifteen years for them to make anything like the effect that was planned. Now, nearly thirty years after they were planted, they are right, to my mind, and make two solid green lines twelve feet high and eighteen feet wide framing the house from the canal.

I wish the Bachelor Duke had resisted altering the steps on the South Front. It was a repetition of his destruction of the First Duke's curved staircase in the Painted Hall. The keystones he mentions, of a satyr, and the other 'as like as if it had been intended for the portrait of a Lady Jane Montague, whose early death we lamented in our youth' is also as like as if it had been intended for the portrait of my sister Unity, whose early death I lament.

The stone table made of a single slab on the perron above came out of the dairy of a farmhouse at Beeley. About twice in a summer it is warm enough to dine out of doors off this table.

Endymion, bronze and naked, lies on his plinth on the lawn below. At a garden party for a women's organisation my mother-in-law heard a lady ask her friend who the statue was of. 'Oh my dear, don't you know? It's Sir Walter Scott' was the surprising answer.

The limes west of the canal have grown to their glorious best in the two hundred years since Dr. Johnson discoursed under them in 1784. Mercifully they were spared in the mighty gale of 1962 when they received and withstood the full force of the west wind.

The Arboretum°

Here, supposing that you are looking at all things with new eyes, you will first perceive, in the health and arrangement of the plants, traces of the management and skill attached to a name that will be for ever connected with Chatsworth, the name of one who has multiplied every attraction it possessed. The creations of his talent are remarkable and conspicuous whichever way you turn. The good sense, benevolence, and simplicity of his character dispose all people well towards him. His boundless enthusiasm for the beautiful and marvellous in nature, controlled by a judgement that is faultless in execution, and a taste that is as refined as it is enterprising and daring, are the cause of increased approbation in those, who observe in his habits and character the most practical, the most zealous, and the least obtrusive of servants. Exciting the good will and praise of the highest and the

Joseph Paxton
(1803–1865) by H.
P. Briggs

lowest, unspoiled and unaltered, he has risen to something like command over all persons who approach him, without one instance of a complaint, or a word said or insinuated against him by anybody, to me, or to any other person. Beloved and blessed by the poor, considered and respected by all. To me a friend, if ever man had one.

Joseph Paxton was born the 3rd of August, 1803. I made his acquaintance in the Horticultural Society's garden at Chiswick, where he was placed in 1823. He was chiefly employed then in training the creepers and newly-introduced plants on the walls there, which first excited my attention; and being in want of a gardener here, I asked Mr. Sabine, who was then at the head of the establishment, whether he thought that young man would do? He said, "young and untried," but spoke so favourably, that I had no doubt.

The young man had made a large lake in 1822 at Sir Gregory Page Turner's place near Woburn. He came to Chatsworth in 1826. You shall have it in his own words. "I left London by the Comet coach for Chesterfield, arrived at Chatsworth at half past four o'clock in the morning of the ninth of May, 1826. As no person was to be seen at that early hour, I got over the greenhouse gate by the old covered way, explored the pleasure-grounds, and

211

looked round the outside of the house. I then went down to the kitchen-gardens, scaled the outside wall, and saw the whole of the place, set the men to work there at six o'clock; then returned to Chatsworth, and got Thomas Weldon to play me the water-works, and afterwards went to breakfast with poor dear Mrs. Gregory and her niece: the latter fell in love with me, and I with her, and thus completed my first morning's work at Chatsworth before nine o'clock."

At the kitchen-garden he found four pine-houses, bad; two vineries, which contained eight bunches of grapes; two good peach-houses, and a few cucumber frames. There were no houses at all for plants, and there was nowhere a plant of later introduction than about the year 1800. There were eight rhododendrons, and not one camellia. He married Miss Sarah Bown in 1827. In a very short time a great change appeared in pleasure-ground and garden: vegetables, of which there had been none, fruit in perfection, and flowers. The twelve men with brooms in their hands on the lawn began to sweep, the labourers to work with activity. The kitchen-garden was so low, and exposed to floods from the river, that I supposed the first wish of the new gardener would be to remove it to some other place—but he made it answer. In 1829 the management of the woods was entrusted to him, and gradually they were rescued from a prospect of destruction. Not till 1823 did I take to caring for my plants in earnest. The old greenhouse was converted into a stove, the greenhouse at the gardens was built, the Arboretum invented and formed. Then started up Orchidaceæ, and three successive houses were built to receive their increasing numbers. In 1835 the intelligent gardener, John Gibson, was despatched to India to secure the Amherstia nobilis, and other treasures of the East. The colossal new Conservatory was invented and begun in 1836; the following year Baron Ludwig was so charmed with its conception, that he stripped his garden at the Cape of the rarest produce of Africa. Paxton had now been employed in the superintendence and formation of my roads; he had made one tour with me in the West of England, and in 1838 contrived to accompany me for an entire year abroad, in which time, having gone through Switzerland and Italy, he trod in Greece, Turkey, Asia Minor, Malta, Spain, and Portugal. In absence he managed that no progress should be checked at home: a great calamity ruined the expedition he had set on foot to California; the unfortunate Wallace and Banks, young gardeners from Chatsworth, having been drowned in Columbia river. He went with me in 1840 to Lismore—and in that year the Conservatory was finished. The village of Edensor was new-

*modelled, and rebuilt, between 1839 and 1841, and now the crowning works
have been the fountains and the rock garden.*

*The Arboretum follows nearly the same line as the old and only walk that
went round the garden. We begin by going down some old steps near the lime-
trees; and, having loyally gazed on the oak planted by the Queen in 1832, her
mother's chestnut, and her husbands's sycamore, we commence this botanical
excursion. It is beautiful as a walk for reference, and for proof of what our
climate will endure, it is a most valuable collection.*

*The shorn laurels are an imitation of Temple Newsam: the cut yews were
large, but very straggling trees; it was in vain to attempt to make them look
very like cypresses; they have rather the appearance of Jacks in the Green on
May Day, and you expect to see them roll over and dance. The walk now
keeps upon a level: it used to follow the sunk fence, and on the other side of
the hollow it was a heavy pull to get up the hill. Being the sole dry walk of the
place, everybody met each other in the course of the day: whether that was
an advantage was as it might be. Keeping our level, we pass a brow of the
hill, once a great scene of gambols, of sledging, not on snow, but on short turf
quite as slippery. The gravel walk below was an effectual check to the rapid
progress, which was invested by the sunk fence below with some appearance
of danger. You pass the heathery roof of an ice-house, and soon after begins
the Arboretum. The plants are classed according to the natural orders of
Jussieu: the names of orders and of plants were painted upon dark-coloured
wooden boards, and appeared rather dismal to a romantic foreigner, when
she said, "Ah! mon Dieu, que c'est touchant! ce sont, sans doute, les
tombeaux des plantes!" and indeed they did look like small Russian grave-
stones. Alas! she and her accomplished sister repose now in the tomb: both
were by birth Princesses of the house of Soltikoff; and farther on is a tree
planted, when here, by the charming Sophia Schouwaloff.*

The oak planted by Queen Victoria in 1832, her mother's chestnut and
her husband's sycamore thrive. Below them, and cleverly hidden, is the
turbine house where electricity for the house was made for forty years
from 1893.

The winding path to the Pinetum is grassed now. Granny planted a
lot of early-flowering rhododendrons behind the Grotto, grown from
seed brought back in 1921 by a Himalayan expedition of Kingdon-
Ward's to which the Duke subscribed. These are big and strong now and
flower well in mild springs.

Returning to the Arboretum, the clear stream, brought with much care from a distance of two miles on the East Moor, here first makes its appearance; the purest water, and a course so natural, that the walk appears to be made for it, not it for the walk. Here is, or ought to be, Luttrell's seat, in the spot he fancied: the style is Saracenic; the columns are of Aberdeen granite, and the rude central capital of serpentino came with me from Palermo, and is the cause of this manner of decoration?

We descend with the brook through a region of chestnuts, oaks, and the hardy class of forest trees, where seedling rhododendrons are beginning to spring up of their own accord. We conclude with the true place of the Pinetum, and a repetition of its finest trees: the Asiatic looking ones, like lofty brooms, are Ashes, grafted from the weeping Ash; and now you join the walk that, passing the foot of the cascade, leads you to the new wonders of the rock garden. I must describe it, not as it is now, but as it will be next year: the progress has been rapid. In the Autumn of 1842 there was not a single stone in these parts; you will now find a labyrinth of rocky walks. Dantan jeune was here at the beginning, and, much puzzled, had the kindness to give us a sketch for the better arrangement of the rocks. He would be surprised to see the structure of which the foundations were then laid. I charge you to take notice of several features of this new work; of the old copper willow-tree re-appearing after a long eclipse, the double flights of steps, with balustrades of Irish yew, the Queen's rock, Prince Albert's, and the Duke of Wellington's last removed and grandest of all. The spirit of some Druid seem to animate Mr. Paxton in these bulky removals. Behold the tremendous Strid, where again figures the clearest of streams, a fac-simile of the renowned chasm of the Wharf, only tamed; and where the saut perilleux may be accomplished without danger or alarm.

The Great Conservatory and the Garden°

You arrive at the Great Conservatory. It is not a thing to be described. Its success has been complete, both for the growth of plants and the enjoyment it affords, being, I believe, the only hothouse known, to remain in which longer than ten minutes does not produce a state of suffering. In consequence also of the subterranean furnaces, to which a railway conducts the coal, there is the remarkable feature of cleanliness, and absence of smoke and smell, unknown in any other building of the kind.

Repairing the Great Conservatory a century ago

You perceive that the situation is perfectly well adapted, being sheltered on all sides by high trees: it was, indeed cleared out of the heart of the wood; yet, strange to say, far as it was from any habitation, traces were discovered underground of walls, and flues much used, and some fragments of fluted columns.

The foundations of the Great Conservatory are all that is left of that famous monument. After its demise two tennis courts were laid in the middle section, but the heating pipes underneath gave way here and there and made holes and hills which annoyed the players. Rather than do the formidable amount of work which would have been necessary to level them properly we changed the scene in 1962 and planted a maze. We chose yews, which grow much faster than is generally thought. It took 1,209 plants, and Dennis Fisher drew the design.

Inside the Great Conservatory just before it was demolished

The north section of the Conservatory garden is planted with dahlias and Michaelmas daisies for the autumn and the south is all lupins. One of the advantages of a very big garden is that you can arrange for bits of it to be in flower all at once and make a really good display, and when it is over it can be forgotten by the visitor till next flowering season. Mop-headed acacias (*Robinia pseudoacacia inermis*) give a little height here and there, and these lovely little trees keep their light spring green till September.

We will now walk round the upper terrace, from which you see to advantage the fine groups of beech and holly that surround it, and you look down upon the column, or pedestal, composed of four circular blocks of marble, which are indeed most interesting, having been part of the Temple of Minerva Sunias: they were brought home by Sir Augustus Clifford; and he had not robbed the shrine, for they had already been rolled down to the sea-beach, where sand and waves would soon have concealed them.

The bust was executed by Campbell without any order, and for twenty years, or more, had encumbered his studio; at last I have relieved him of it, and it is to encounter the storms of the Peak in this exposed situation. But certainly no bust ever had so grand a pedestal.

After the gale of 1962

Following the Bachelor Duke to the upper terrace you meet his marble pillar from Sunion with the bronze bust of him by Campbell on it. This was always its place, but when we came here there was no path to it through the wood. I thought it should have an approach of importance, but could not decide on how to do it till I saw the serpentine wall at Hopton Hall near Wirksworth, and that seemed the right kind of shape. A wall was out of the question, so we planted a serpentine hedge of beech from the Ring Pond up to and enclosing the statue. Here again it looked hopelessly out of scale when it was planted eighteen inches high in 1953, and we had to wait twenty years before it began to look right. In the gale of 1962 five forest trees fell across it, and the poor Bachelor Duke toppled off his column and his good old head lay in a sorry mess of branches and twigs at its base. He was unhurt, and the squashed beeches were replaced, so a year later it was impossible to see the damage done by the wind.

We walk back to the far end of the canal and you must pause to look at the south front of the house and remark the work of some unknown

217

genius who caused the lawn to be set a few inches lower than the canal so from here the house looks as if it rises out of the water.

We again go down the limetree steps, and make a farther descent into the West Garden. This space, flanked by the two large bastions, from its size was difficult to fill and adorn, but Sir Jeffry Wyatville's most ingenious architectural parterres have gone a great way towards it, and the Tulip fountain has lately given life and animation to the centre. The whole forms a support and a platform, that connect and harmonize the buildings of Chatsworth to the utmost advantage. Here stand two imperial trees, planted by the brothers Nicolas and Michael Paulowitsch; the first, a Spanish chestnut, promises to be of surpassing beauty.

I shall not undertake to lead you through the kitchen garden: the botanical treasures there require a more able and technical description than I can give, and the fruit-trees and vegetables, that rival them in perfection, would increase the difficulty of the task; but when you have been there, when you have visited the Stand and the new fountain-reservoir, when you have been round the four mile walk, and have examined the villages of Calton Lees and Edensor, paying great attention to the farm, you will have revived the most thorough acquaintance with Chatsworth and what surrounds it; and you will make allowances for the excess of pride, vanity, egotism—call it what you please—that have made me dwell upon such minute particulars in complying with your request. To enjoy such sources of happiness, and to see the pleasure they cause to others, would make it as impossible to treat them with indifference, as it is to deserve the possession of them.

Now we go towards the house under Dr Johnson's limes and down the steps into the West Garden. Sir Jeffry's 'architectural parterres' used to be filled with bedded-out plants, never very satisfactory, and I am much more pleased with the new scheme of sharp geometrical patterns of box which fit very well with the old golden yew cushions at each corner and a new clipped yew in the middle.

The long narrow garden is a funnel for the north wind, so Andrew decided to cut it into three with yew hedges. The middle division was a problem. It is important, because all the west windows of the house look down on it. There was a wretched muddle of shrubs in the four corners, a motley collection of a specially unattractive pink prunus, junipers and cupressus. Inspiration for this place came when I was looking at an exhibition of the architectural plans of Chiswick House, Lord

Burlington's perfect little palace on the outskirts of London. It struck me that the circle of the dome was about the same size as the round pond, and from then on it was simple. We copied the plan of walls, stairs and pillars, and it is only one foot out of scale. It was planted in golden box, 3,350 of them, golden because the dark climate of Derbyshire needs any lightening it can get. When they were ordered the nurseryman said, 'No one has wanted *that* since 1914.' The design must be looked down on from above. It is meaningless, except for children to steeplechase over, when you are on its own level.

In the same year (1960) a new tennis court was made at the south end of this garden hidden by a high hedge of horse-chestnuts. An opening was made in the wall, and for the first time it was possible to get vehicles in the West Garden. Until then all machines, implements, plants and manure had to be taken up and down the steps on ramps. The border directly opposite the house was widened and steps up to it constructed in the middle. The lions' heads came from a cottage near Buxton. The stone table was demanded by Paddy Leigh-Fermor, who complained there was nowhere to write out of doors, and the stone seat was moved from the Conservatory Garden.

I think a very big garden demands something alive and moving in it. Various heavy breeds of poultry are at large near the greenhouses. Buff Cochins and Dark Brahmas, with their extravagantly feathered legs and feet wander about there.

So we come to the end of the tour of the garden, but we shall never come to the end of the battle with nature which is gardening, the outdoor housework of weeding, mowing and tidying up, or the pleasure of the days when everything is right, when the wind goes down and the smell of azaleas takes over, when the first roses come out, when the bees are on the lime flowers, or when the butterflies crowd round the Michaelmas daisies on a still autumn day.

The Park°

The land which is enclosed by a deer fence nine miles long has undergone many changes in appearance. As you see it now it is largely the creation of the Fourth Duke (1720–1764) who razed some of the village of Edensor on the west side of the river and enclosed more land in that direction.* He engaged Lancelot (Capability) Brown to plant it in the apparently 'natural' fashion of the time.

The afforestation of the steep bank behind the house, Stand Wood, followed, and is almost an extension of the garden in that it merges with it, and you cannot see where the garden ends and the wood begins when you take in the whole picture from the drive west of the river. The Bachelor Duke and Paxton completed the unification of garden and wood when they enclosed further parkland at the south end of the garden to make the Pinetum.

The public road (B 6012) was made about 1770. Till then the tracks ran east-west, and many of them can still be seen. It is very unusual for a public road to run through the park of a big house, and I think it is one of the blessings of Chatsworth, because travellers are made to feel welcome by the lack of high walls and locked gates as soon as they cross the grids on to the unfenced road. To drive through the park invites you to return and have a longer look and walk on the old turf grazed hard by sheep and deer so it is like an endless lawn, and to see the house, river, woods and village of Edensor from new directions where every prospect pleases.

People have always been welcome to walk, to bring their children and dogs, picnic and play games in the park wherever and whenever they like. No matter what the time of year or how awful the weather there are always people about. When Emma was about fourteen and immersed in all things Russian we looked out of the window one dreary wet winter afternoon and saw a crowd crossing the bridge. It was the time when people started buying special clothes to walk in, and the damp parade of bright anoraks, woolly hats and socks and laced-up boots in the November gloom was something new and surprising. 'Look, Mum, Ivan the Terrible's men', she said.

The only private bit is the Old Park, where the red and fallow deer can hide their calves and fawns in the bracken under the ancient oaks and keep their own essential privacy.

The oaks are the scattered outliers of the western edge of Sherwood Forest. They are gnarled relics of the time when the greater part of the Midlands was covered by trees and 'a squirrel could travel from the

---

*The few remaining houses which could be seen from Chatsworth were pulled down in the 1830s. The Bachelor Duke then rebuilt the village, and it is little changed since then.

Severn to the Humber without touching the ground'. There is much speculation as to their age. My father-in-law thought some must be nearly a thousand years old, those which have enormous boles but are only kept alive now by a few small branches with leaves. He said they would have been five hundred years growing to their best and five hundred years going back to their present state.

In 1945 an oak (not one of the giants) was blown down and taken to the yard of Messrs Allen & Orr in Chesterfield for conversion. When it was sawn up a ball shot was found embedded in the timber. A ring count revealed that over four hundred years' growth enclosed the shot, and on the inner side the timber was so decayed as to render the rings uncountable.

The girth of the biggest of these forest kings measures twenty-five feet nine inches at four feet three inches from the ground. We plant about thirty English oaks (*Quercus robur*), and no other species, in the Old Park every year.

The name of Robin Hood crops up in several local landmarks. One is Robin Hood's Seat, the highest rock above the Old Park. There is a legend that he shot an arrow from here to decide where he should be buried. It landed in Hathersage, eight and a half miles away as the arrow flies, where Little John's grave is indeed in the churchyard.

Till 1823 the Baslow (north) end of the park belonged to the Duke of Rutland. It was added through an exchange of land that year. The lodges at the Turret Gates (sometimes called the Golden Gates, though they are pitch black now) were built in 1842 to designs left by Wyatville, who died in 1841. The splendid wrought iron work was originally the Fifth Duke's West Terrace gates, and arrived here in 1843, probably at the suggestion of Decimus Burton. Their matching pair is in the central arch of the north screen of the house.

When I first got to know the park during and just after the Second World War there were no divisions and no grids to stop the cattle going out on to the road. They could leave the park over the One Arch bridge at the Beeley end and by Tea Pot Row at Edensor, and when the gate into the village was left open (which it very often was) they wandered up the lane towards Bakewell. Everyone expected this to happen, and the gardens were arranged to keep out cattle, sheep and deer, all fenced and gated. Driving the cattle back into the park along the main road was an almost daily chore, but in the days when people walked or bicycled and were not encapsulated in a car, there was usually someone about to do it. The grid was made at the entrance to Edensor in 1948, but the two on the main road were not constructed till 1959. After that there were no more wild rushes up the road.

In 1948 the park was divided into three by a fence and grid on the private drive near Queen Mary's Bower and a second fence from the garden to the river south of the house. It was done so that both tuberculin tested cattle and those not tested could run in the park but could not meet.

In June 1963 President Kennedy came to England to see Uncle Harold, then Prime Minister. He broke his journey to Birch Grove to visit the grave of his sister Kathleen in Edensor churchyard. The Presidential plane, Air Force 1, arrived at a military airfield in Lincolnshire and he came from there in a helicopter and landed in the park close to the churchyard. American security men had been here for days checking every detail. They asked me what sort of people lived in Edensor, their names and how long they had lived there, and were incredulous when the answers were, 'Fifty years, I should think,' or 'He was born here, and I suppose he's about 70.'

Although it was not planned, Jack Kennedy came to the house and walked up the West Stairs where the unsuspecting visitors on a quiet afternoon were astonished to see the President of the United States. The day after he had been here I asked one of the lifelong inhabitants of Edensor what he thought about it. 'Not much. The wind from that machine blew my chickens away, and I haven't seen them since.'

Many of the people in Edensor and Beeley were smallholders and kept a cow or two as well as the usual pig. The fields above Edensor each have a stone shed where the cow and young stock were wintered, but in the summer they were grazed in the park, so the field could be shut up for hay.

Mr Sam Burdekin (*b.* 1888), formerly a farm worker and later a tenant-farmer, told me, 'When I was young we kept a cow. Practically all the people kept one. About a dozen people would walk out of Beeley to the Blue Doors [the lodge at the south end of the Old Park] morning and night to milk the cows, and that happened at Edensor and Baslow as well. They would go on to the milking hillock where the cows would be waiting for them. They used to divide the milk and make cheese. One would have it one day and then the others.'

There was a Cow Club at Pilsley founded in 1862, and the owners paid a few shillings a year as insurance against the death of their beast. It was still going in the 1930s.

Mrs Tindale of Beeley (*b.* 1893) told me her grandmother (who was one of a big family of girls worked by their father as if they were boys) had to milk in the morning then take a load of stone from Burnt Wood quarry above Beeley to Chatsworth, take another load of stone in the afternoon and milk again in the evening. This was in the 1820s when the North Wing was being built. Mrs Tindale's granddaughter Christine is housekeeper at Chatsworth now, so it was her great-great-grandmother who carted the stone to build where Christine's flat is now.

Till the 1950s there were several acres of neatly raked allotments at Beeley, and at Pilsley and Edensor each holder had his own entrance gate off the road. Although the people who live in those villages are nearly all keen gardeners, the allotments (with one notable exception) are no longer worked and have been put down to grass.

The Stand Wood°

Although this steep and rocky bank was planted with hardwood in the eighteenth century the walks which cross and re-cross the drive to the Hunting Tower and Park Farm were laid out by Paxton, and he added many conifers, some newly introduced to the British Isles. It was he who planted *Rhododendron ponticum* here, that horrible, hardy and invasive shrub which spreads with alarming speed in lime-free soil and must be kept in check if it is not to take over from everything else.

It blocked up the paths, and even Holmes Lane, the ancient pack-horse track which was once the main road to the moor and Chesterfield, was impassable. They were cleared in 1976, and the forest floor is once again pleasant to walk on. We have cut down trees here and there to allow the huge views to the west, across the Derwent valley to the Peak District and its white stone walls.

Three big monkey puzzles (*Araucaria imbricata*) set one wondering what the Bachelor's line of them along the broad walk east of the house must have looked like. Perhaps it is as well they disappeared before

Andrew came on the scene, as I can imagine what the pressures would have been as to whether or not to cut them down.

Replanting in the Stand Wood is by natural regeneration or standard trees. Many old and decaying trees, which would have no place in commercial woodlands, are left on purpose, as the insects which live in and on them provide food for the birds; and the holes in unsound wood also provide nesting-places for birds from tits to owls. While there are keepers to control the vermin (now called Wild Life and fed by old ladies in suburbs) there will be an abundance of songbirds in these woods and in the garden. They are one of the great joys of this place.

Above the wood is an area of flat ground where there are four large man-made lakes, the reservoirs for the waterworks in the garden. For a century they supplied the water which worked the hydraulic machines in the old building yard (now the Farmyard) and later to the turbine house.

The Swiss Lake is the oldest of these, dug to provide water for the Cascade in the last years of the seventeenth century. In 1839 the Swiss Cottage was built at the water's edge on the east side of the pond, a very pretty addition to a very pretty place.

The story of the Emperor Lake and the fountain it feeds is a tribute to the genius of Paxton. When the Duke was in Russia in 1843 he greatly admired the fountain he saw at Peterhof, and determined to have a bigger and better one at Chatsworth to surprise the Czar, who promised to stay with him when he came to England the following year.

Accordingly Paxton set to work on a job after his own heart where his talent for engineering had full play. Having an abundant supply of water at a considerable height above the garden the possibilities of using it to make displays of gravity-fed waterworks were endless, but it had to be stored and harnessed to its work. Paxton started his survey in December 1843 to determine the different levels. A conduit two and a half miles long was dug across the moor to drain water into the new reservoir west of the existing Swiss Lake and 350 feet above the house.

The digging of the lake was a major task. It covers eight acres and 100,000 cubic yards of earth was moved by men and horses and the banks were lined with stone. Its average depth is seven feet. 'I walked up with Paxton to see the new reservoir, half frightened by the immense work,' wrote the Duke.

The question of the supply to the fountain itself is set out in Paxton's *Magazine of Botany* of 1844, dedicated by him to the Czar:

Much consideration was given to the nature of the pipes which were to convey the water from the reservoir, down the sloping hill to the fountain, in order that, while security and strength might be obtained on the one hand, no unnecessary waste of metal might be occasioned on the other. Various hydraulic and pneumatic experiments were made, so as to arrive at a proper conclusion on the important part of the business. The results appeared so perfectly satisfactory to Mr. Paxton that he at once fixed upon the various forms and dimensions and the work commenced.

The pipe selected was of 15 in. bore and a maximum of $1\frac{1}{2}$ in. thick. The pipe joints were turned and bored, with clip sockets for additional security. The total fall was 381 ft. including 200 ft. at 1 in 2 so it was necessary to cut a trench out of solid rock 15 feet deep in places, and two ponds had to be crossed as well.

Near the fountains was a double-acting valve, which took 5 minutes to open or close fully, so that shock damage to the pipes could be avoided. The nozzles of the jet were made of brass, and the normal jet would play 267 ft. and is on record as having reached 296 ft.

The worked progressed at great speed in the winter of 1843–4, continuing at night by the light of flares, and it was duly ready on time — only six months after it was begun. Alas, the Czar never came to Chatsworth, but it was called the Emperor Fountain in his honour, and is a rare sight to this day.

The nine-acre Swiss Lake and the two-and-a-half-acre Ring Pond are used when necessary to top up the Emperor. As well as supplying the fountain, water from the latter flows over the waterfall, the aqueduct and down the cascade in the garden to the River Derwent below.

In the last thirty-five years there have been two notable changes out of doors. It no longer gets dark now, because of the virulent street lights in Baslow, and there is never silence, except in a fog or on Christmas morning.

Epilogue

The charm, attraction, character, call it what you will, of the house is that it has grown over the years in a haphazard sort of way. Nothing fits exactly, none of the rooms except the Chapel is a set-piece, like those in many houses which were built and furnished by one man in the fashion of one time. It is a conglomeration of styles and periods, of furniture and decoration. You find a hideous thing next to a beautiful thing, and since taste is intensely personal you would probably disagree with me as to which is which. It is a decorator's nightmare, unless that decorator has exceptionally catholic taste. There is no theme, no connecting style. Each room is a jumble of old and new, English and foreign, thrown together by generations of acquisitive inhabitants and standing up to change by the variety of its proportions and the strength of its cheerful atmosphere.

Likewise the outside. There is something surprising to see wherever you look; nothing can be taken for granted. Some of the house is like a mongrel dog, bits too long and bits too short, a beautiful head with an out of scale tail, and in the garden there are buildings and ornaments of so many dates and tastes you begin to wonder who was in charge here and when.

It has all been done by the confident dictators of yesteryear with no recourse to committees or wondering what other people will think about their additions and subtractions.

It is sad to see the decline in confidence of the architectural profession and their patrons in the twentieth-century. Can you imagine one of the giants of the seventeenth or eighteenth century showing his client a plan with a lot of little trees dotted about to distract the eye from the nasty building he has drawn? It seems to be the practice now to add whitebeams and birches, till the architect turns into the Old Man Sitting on a Gate in *Alice Through the Looking Glass*, who said:

> And I was thinking of a plan
> To dye one's whiskers green,
> And always use so large a fan
> That they could not be seen.

Sometimes the fan is a bull-dozed bank, but even that has to be planted with half-hearted trees and shrubs, never a proper oak or beech. I wonder if it is all done in an office, or if they go outside like John Fowler did when he became as interested in gardens as he was in curtains: he used to leave his client in the drawing-room and go into the garden, stop and raise his arms above his head shouting, 'I'm a lime.' The client was supposed to know if he was in the right place and had the rare chance to assert his authority by moving him a foot or two to right or left. Then John would throw himself on the ground in an attitude of prayer murmuring, 'I'm prostrate rosemary.' He never suggested birches or whitebeams.

I know there is the great new difficulty of fitting in water, electricity, central heating, lifts, telephones, baths, lavatories and even air-conditioning, which did not worry Palladio and his successors, but I guess he and they would have made a better fist of the finished article.

Architects are also constrained by law and have to consult officials at every step.

It would have been an exquisite pleasure to see the Bachelor Duke confronted by the Planning Officer, or Paxton with a wet towel round his head studying the Standard Code of Practice and Building Management, or the First Duke and Talman oiling up to the Building Inspector. Perhaps that Duke would have been provoked into tweaking another nose and earning an even larger fine than the £30,000 he owed for assaulting poor Colonel Culpepper.

How surprised the Fifth Duke would be to learn that he could not now build his red brick hotel at Edensor; but neither would he be allowed to pull it down.

The combined brains of Thomas Hobbes and Henry Cavendish might have been able to get the hang of the rules, but they are baffling indeed to an ordinary mortal.

The builders of Chatsworth were not encumbered by regulations. I think they did it very well.

The endless variety of work inside and out, and the pleasure of working with people who love this place make life here very agreeable.

There is too much to do, which is good. I often feel like one of my sisters who says she hasn't got time to cut her toenails, and my favourite aunt who said on her eightieth birthday 'I'm not afraid of dying. What I can't bear is the thought of eternal rest.'

Index

Figures in italics indicate a reference to an illustration (on the facing page if it is colour). The main references to parts of the house described in Part Two come first even if there are other earlier references.

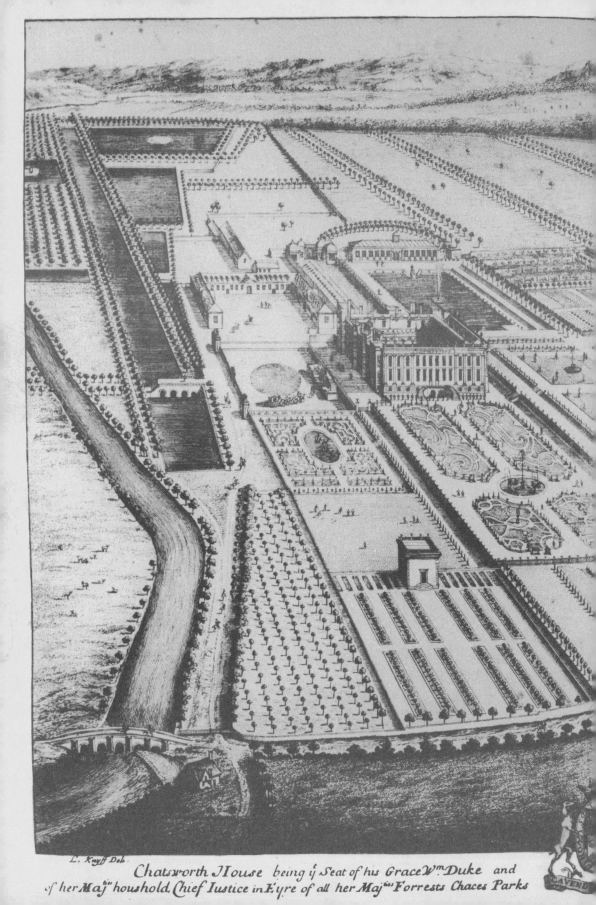

L. Kuyff Del.

Chatsworth House being ÿ Seat of his Grace W.ᵐ Duke and
of her Maᵗᵗⁱᵉ houshold. Chief Iustice in Eyre of all her Maᵗⁱᵉˢ Forrests Chaces Parks